The Parameters of Postmodernism

THE PARAMETERS OF POSTMODERNISM

Nicholas Zurbrugg

SOUTHERN ILLINOIS UNIVERSITY PRESS

Carbondale and Edwardsville

Library of Congress Cataloging-in-Publication Data

Zurbrugg, Nicholas.
  The parameters of postmodernism / Nicholas Zurbrugg.
      p.   cm.
  Includes index.
  1. Postmodernism (Literature) 2. Postmodernism. I. Title.
PN98.P67Z87   1993
809'.04—dc20   92-20003
  ISBN 0-8093-1852-0
  ISBN 0-8093-1887-3 (pbk.)   CIP

The paper used in this publication meets the minimum requirements of American National Standard for Information
Sciences—Permanence of Paper for Printed Library Materials, ANSI Z39.48-1984. ⊚

To the memory of John Cage ❏

Contents ❏

Contents

Contents

Preface ❏

So many books have been written about postmodern culture
that it may seem imprudent to add to their number. On the
other hand, so many studies of the cultural climate of the last
half century narrowly dwell upon the alleged "postmodern crisis" in Europe and America that it is time for the wider parameters of postmodernism to be identified.

This book takes as its starting point the hypothesis that the
present tendency to define postmodern culture negatively, in
terms of "schizophrenia," "superficiality," and so forth, derives
from overliteral and undercritical responses to some of the more
seductive overstatements by European theorists such as Benjamin, Barthes, Bürger, Baudrillard, Bonito-Oliva, and Bourdieu. It identifies this tendency with the *B-effect* mythology or
the apocalyptic register informing most European and American writings on postmodernism.

The morbid enthusiasm of B-effect converts obsessed with
the apparent neutrality, decline, stagnation, submonumental-
ity, and general obsolescence of creativity in present times is
decidedly symptomatic of *one* facet of the postmodern mentality.
So indeed are the pages of *National Enquirer, Mad*, and *Vanity
Fair*. Flat-earthers have also had their day and may well live
to do so once again. Nevertheless, other more rewarding facets
of postmodern culture also exist, and if so many cartographers
of postmodern creativity fail to perceive them, then, as the
American performance artist Laurie Anderson suggests, this is
perhaps "because they're looking for it in the wrong place." In
Anderson's terms, "for anyone to say that creativity is dead just
says that this particular person is creatively dead."[1]

As this book attempts to demonstrate, the literary and artis-

Preface

tic temper of the postmodern condition in Europe and America cannot adequately be understood unless one complements B-effect generalizations with the more positive implications of the innovative creative practices that I associate with the *C-effect* characterizing the multimedia experiments of the American composer John Cage and other avant-garde artists.

In America these artists include Laurie Anderson, Robert Ashley, Philip Glass, Meredith Monk, Yvonne Rainer, and Robert Wilson; in Europe, technological artists such as the sound poet Henri Chopin, the telematics pioneer Roy Ascott, and the kinetic and electronic artists documented in Frank Popper's memorable *Electra* exhibition at the Paris Musée d'Art Moderne in 1983. A second European variant of the C-effect informs the ways in which artists and writers such as Umberto Eco, Günter Grass, Christa Wolf, Joseph Beuys, and Heiner Müller all attempt to negotiate the future by combining more traditional past and present discourses. The collaborations between Heiner Müller and Robert Wilson offer particularly striking evidence of the ways in which current cultural traditions now transcend temporal, geographical, verbal, ideological, and technological borders.

These pages are written very much in the spirit of the "far-flung intertextuality" that Anna Balakian has associated with my earlier work,[2] offering a succession of strategic deliberations upon what I sense to be the most telling contradictions within B-effect scholarship and the most exciting innovations within C-effect creativity.

Hopefully they will encourage the reader to look beyond the platitudes of B-effect accounts of postmodern culture and to consider present practices in a more critical and discriminating manner. Throughout this book I have attempted to refer directly to primary rather than secondary material, and I base much of the latter part of my argument upon my own interviews with the artists and writers in question. Postmodern culture requires empirical analysis.

Preface

Notes

1. Laurie Anderson, interview with author, 8 June 1991.
2. Anna Balakian, review of *Dada Spectrum: The Dialectics of Revolt*, ed. Stephen C. Foster and Rudolf E. Kuenzli (Madison, Wis.: Coda, 1979), *L'Esprit Créateur* 20.3 (Fall 1980): 99.

Acknowledgments ❑

I am particularly grateful to the Faculty of Humanities, Griffith University, for its continued generous financial support for my research.

I would like to offer my acknowledgment to Robert Lax for permission to reproduce his poem "A Problem in Design" (first published in his *Fables*, ed. Emil Antonucci [New York: Journeyman Press, 1970]).

I would like to acknowledge permission from Carcanet Press Limited to reproduce lines from Edwin Morgan's translation of Bertolt Brecht's poem "A Worker Reads, and Asks These Questions" (collected in Edwin Morgan's *Rites of Passage* [(Manchester, Eng.: Carcanet Press, 1976]).

I would further like to acknowledge permission from Chris Mann to quote from SCRATCH SCRATCH *(A history of grammar)* from *Allos: 'Other' Language,* collected and assembled by Kenneth Gaburo, Iowa City: Lingua Press, 1980, p. 231.

It gives me great pleasure to thank all the artists and writers who have shared their time and ideas with me, particularly: Kathy Acker, Laurie Anderson, Robert Ashley, J. G. Ballard, Jean Baudrillard, Samuel Beckett, Hans Breder, William Burroughs, Warren Burt, John Cage, Henri Chopin, Bob Cobbing, Ian Hamilton Finlay, Kenneth Gaburo, John Giorno, Philip Glass, Brion Gysin, Jenny Holzer, Tim Johnson, Barbara Kruger, Robert Lax, Barry McCallion, Jackson MacLow, Chris Mann, Meredith Monk, Yvonne Rainer, Steve Reich, Edite Vidins, David Warrilow, Larry Wendt, Robert Wilson, Adam Wolter, and Ellen Zweig.

I am also extremely grateful to my friends and colleagues who have wittingly or unwittingly directed or redirected these

Acknowledgments

pages upon their way: Peter Anderson, Vincent Barras, David Briers, Rex Butler, Joanne Canary, Graham Coulter-Smith, Stephen Crofts, Vera Daniel, David de Giustino, John Fletcher, Sarah Follent, Dieter Freundlieb, James Grauerholz, Michele Helmrich, Wayne Hudson, Rudolph Kuenzli, Eric Michaels, Christopher Norris, Robert Scanlan, Urszula Szulakowska, Martin Travers, Nicholas Tsoutas, and Tony Wilson.

I owe more gratitude than I can say to Diana Solano, miracle worker, for preserving equilibrium and processing pages almost as fast as they materialized during my writing frenzy of summer 1991. Likewise, I am indebted to Karen Yarrow and Robyn Pratten for patiently and meticulously keeping subsequent words in line.

My thanks, too, to my editors at Southern Illinois University Press, Carol A. Burns and Curtis Clark, and to Rebecca Spears Schwartz, who copyedited this volume's final format.

To my mother in Kersey, to my brothers Michael and Anthony in London, Max and Hanne Liebmann in New York, and to Larry Wendt in San Jose, I offer my continued gratitude for welcoming this wanderer, around the year, around the globe.

Lest I appear ungrateful, I should also like to thank Fredric Jameson for his pages' constant irritation and inspiration: blessings this volume perhaps partially reciprocates in quality and in kind.

Finally, with deep gratitude, respect, and admiration, I offer this book belatedly to John Cage, first and foremost of postmodern artists, and most enlivening and inspiring of guides to our culture's positive parameters.

Anti-Art or Ante-Art? ❑

> Americans have a special horror of giving up
> control, of letting things happen in their own
> way without interference. They would like to
> jump down into their stomachs and digest the
> food and shovel the shit out.
>
> *—William Burroughs*

> I'm able to analyse . . . a text with the computer,
> so that I have a list of all the words throughout
> the source that satisfy the mesostic rules, and
> then, through the use of chance operations, to
> write a text which comes first from here and
> then from there. And I find it very fascinating
> . . . because though it comes from ideas, it pro-
> duces other ideas. There comes a kind of fertil-
> ization of ideas.
>
> *—John Cage*

As Burroughs and Cage suggest,[1] postmodern culture seems
to be characterized by conflict between creators and theorists
who have "a special horror of giving up control" and anticrea-
tors and antitheorists who prefer to combine rules and chance
operations, "letting things happen in their own way." The very
names *Cage* and *Burroughs* have become synonymous with
compositional anarchy—with what post-Spenglerians might
think of as the further and still more irremediable decline of
the West—and with the apparent crises of representation and
legitimation afflicting postmodern culture as a whole.

Yet as Cage helpfully hints, postmodern culture has a surprising capacity to precipitate creative fertilization in strange,
unexpected ways, which may come "first from here and then
from there." Considered in terms of Renato Poggioli's distinction between modes of "*anti*-creation" and modes of "*ante*-cre-
ation,"[2] it makes best sense to consider the parameters of postmodern culture both in terms of the negative and neutralizing
traits that contribute to its *anti*-art (and one should add, its
*anti*theory) and in terms of those "very fascinating" modes of

1

experimentation that testify to postmodernity's proliferation of *ante*-art (or those seemingly negative works that in fact annunciate new modes of positive creativity).

While artists and writers and multimedia creators contributing to postmodern modes of ante-art seem to have little doubt about the positive creative potential of their era, it is only recently that theorists of postmodernity have tentatively admitted that all may not be quite so bleak as most theory stories have assumed. Fredric Jameson, reassessing his previous reservations regarding postmodern practices—in an interview with Anders Stephanson published in the December 1986/January 1987 issue of *Flash Art*—postulates that both postmodern theory and postmodern art *may* explore modes of new space. "It's certainly wrong to go down the list of contemporary trends and once again, in typical leftwing fashion, try and find out which is progressive. The only way through a crisis of space is to invent a new space."[3]

Taking this hypothesis one step further, Jameson concedes that certain American postmoderns have discovered and explored something substantially original within the traditional and the technological arts.

> Warhol is emblematic of one feature of Postmodernism and the same goes for Paik. They allow you to analyze and specify something partial, and in that sense their activities are surely original: they have identified a whole range of things to do and then moved in to colonize this new space.[4]

To some extent, then, Jameson shares Poggioli's recognition of the experimental gesture which, as ante-art, is partial and new rather than completely realized, completely comprehensible, and no longer new. Beckett qualifies such works as "refreshingly strange."[5] Benjamin discusses ante-art in terms of its propensity to create "a demand that could fully be satisfied only later."[6] And Barthes likewise identifies modes of multimedia innovation "born technically, occasionally even aesthetically," long before their advanced evolution allows them to be "born theoretically."[7]

Ironically, Jameson appears unwilling to admit that modes

of postmodern ante-art could—or indeed, even *should*—transmute from ante-art to art. Postmodern art, he reasons, should remain something like a permanently pimpled aesthetic adolescent. For postmodernity, according to Jamesonian logic, is axiomatically incompatible with maturity, permanence, and any aspiration toward *monumentality*. Pondering upon postmodern texts in general and then upon videotexts in particular, Jameson concludes,

> For to talk about any single one of these postmodernist texts is to reify it, to turn it into the work of art it no longer is, to endow it with a permanence and monumentality that is its vocation to dispel. A critic supposed to analyze individual texts is thus faced with insuperable problems: the moment you analyze a single piece of video art you do it violence, you remove some of its provisionality and anonymity and turn it into a masterpiece or at least a privileged text again.[8]

Notes

1. William Burroughs, *Dead Fingers Talk* (London: John Calder, 1963), 20. All subsequent references to this work appear in the text. John Cage, interview with author, *Eyeline* (Brisbane), no. 1 (May 1987): 7. Cage refers to his "fifty per cent mesostics" made from texts by Jasper Johns. An example is published with this interview.
2. Renato Poggioli, *The Theory of the Avant-Garde*, trans. Gerald Fitzgerald (Cambridge: Harvard Univ. Press, Belknap Press, 1968), 136–37. All subsequent references to this work appear in the text.
3. Fredric Jameson, interview with Anders Stephanson, *Flash Art* (international ed.), no. 131 (Dec. 1986/Jan. 1987): 72.
4. Jameson, *Flash Art*, 72.
5. Samuel Beckett, note to the author, 18 Apr. 1981, concerning a record of sound poetry by the French poets Henri Chopin and Bernard Heidsieck, published in *Stereo Headphones* (Brisbane), no. 8-9-10 (1982): 80.
6. Walter Benjamin, "The Work of Art in the Age of Mechanical Reproduction" (1936), in *Illuminations*, trans. Harry Zohn (1955; rpt., Glasgow: Collins, 1979), 239. All subsequent references to this essay appear in the text.
7. Roland Barthes, "The Third Meaning," in *Image-Music-*

Text, trans. Stephen Heath (Glasgow: Collins/Fontana, 1977), 67.

8. Jameson, *Flash Art,* 72.

Monumental Art or
Submonumental Art? ❑

One wonders why postmodern art should be predefined as something provisional, anonymous, or submonumental. Postmodern artists are not the untouchables of world culture any more than postmodern theorists such as Jameson are necessarily the untouchables of cultural theory. In this respect, Jameson appears to be the victim of his own rhetoric, addicted as it were, to the "Word Authority" that William Burroughs describes as "more habit forming than heroin."[1] Put more plainly, Jameson is blinded by the light of his theoretical coordinates. Having subscribed for so long to the myth that postmodernist culture is necessarily provisional, anonymous, and submonumental, Jameson appears bewildered when art resists such categories.

It is all the more ironic that Jameson's earlier writings warn the reader of precisely this problem. Diagnosing his own disease, as it were, within the "increasingly total system or logic" of "the Foucault of the prisons book," Jameson perceptively observes,

> Insofar as the theorist wins, therefore, by constructing an increasingly closed and terrifying machine, to that very degree he loses, since the critical capacity of his work is thereby paralysed, and the impulses of negation and revolt, not to speak of those of social transformation, are increasingly perceived as vain and trivial in the face of the model itself.[2]

Arguably, the "increasingly closed and terrifying" assumptions of Jameson's machine prevent him from perceiving the permanent, personal, and monumental potential of postmodern creativity. Indeed, in the face of his model, the highly provocative and extremely significant "impulses of negation and revolt" of the modernist avant-garde appear equally vain. Justifying his own worst fears, Jameson dismisses dadaism as "the trivial irreverence of Dada,"[3] rather than heeding Benjamin's more perspicacious allusion to the dada artists' aspiration to the "new art form" ("Work of Art," 239) that we now witness in the experiments of Nam June Paik and the other postmodernist innovators that Jameson persists in treating as provisional, anonymous, and so on.

Notes

1. William Burroughs, "Word Authority More Habit Forming Than Heroin," *San Francisco Earthquake* 1.1 (Fall 1967): 25.
2. Fredric Jameson, "Postmodernism, or the Cultural Logic of Late Capitalism," *New Left Review*, no. 146 (July/Aug. 1984): 57.
3. Fredric Jameson, "Hans Haacke and the Cultural Logic of Postmodernism," in *Hans Haacke: Unfinished Business*, ed. Brian Wallis (New York: New Museum of Contemporary Art, 1986), 38.

Eagleton and the Apocalyptic Fallacy ❏

Terry Eagleton exemplifies the same contradictions in his considerations of postmodernist culture. On the one hand, Eagleton convincingly condemns the *apocalyptic* impulse in continental postmodern theory, observing:

> A whole traditional ideology of representation is in crisis, yet this does not mean that the search for truth is abandoned. Postmodernism, by contrast, commits the apocalyptic error of believing that the discrediting of this particular representational epistemology is the death of truth itself, just as it sometimes mistakes the disintegration of certain traditional ideologies of the subject for the subject's disappearance. In both cases the obituary notices are greatly exaggerated.[1]

On the other hand, Eagleton indulges in precisely this kind of apocalyptic fallacy when tried beyond patience by some of postmodernism's more provocative gestures. Mistaking morsels of postmodernism's mischievous bark for the entirety of its bite, Eagleton summarily dismisses Carl Andre's "pile of bricks in the Tate Gallery" (without even bothering to mention Andre's name) and then condemns postmodern culture as a whole in the following exaggerated "obituary notice."

> The depthless, styleless, dehistoricized, decathected surfaces of postmodernist culture are not meant to signify an alienation, for the very concept of alienation must secretly posit a dream of authenticity which postmodernism finds quite unintelligible. Those flattened surfaces and hollowed interiors are not "alienated" because there is no longer any subject to be alienated and nothing to be alienated from, "authenticity" having been less rejected than merely forgotten. ("Capitalism, Modernism," 61)

This is absurdly reductive, and Eagleton should have known better than to take the clichés of superficial postmodern theory and of superficial postmodern creativity quite so seriously. As Roland Barthes suggests in his essay on "The Image" (1978), totalizing judgments tend to arise from, and then become blinkered within, "complete systems" that "*initially* . . . have an [effective] function of counter-Stupidity" but "subsequently . . . become stupid."[2]

Barthes concludes, "Once they 'take,' there is stupidity. . . . One feels like going elsewhere: '*Ciao! No, thanks!*'" While Barthes's successive writings refreshingly evade their own successive systems, bidding them "*Ciao! No, thanks!*" and placing spanner after spanner in the works of their potentially closed machine, Jameson, Eagleton, and other critics of postmodern culture seem less flexible in their assumptions. In Lyotard's terms, they tend to "stifle the systems or subsystems they control" and "asphyxiate themselves in the process."[3]

Notes

1. Terry Eagleton, "Capitalism, Modernism and Postmodernism," *New Left Review*, no. 152 (July/Aug. 1985): 70. All subsequent references to this article appear in the text.
2. Roland Barthes, "The Image," in *The Rustle of Language*, trans. Richard Howard (New York: Hill and Wang, 1986), 351.
3. Jean-François Lyotard, *The Postmodern Condition: A Re-*

port on Knowledge, trans. Geoff Bennington and Brian Massumi, with foreword by Fredric Jameson (Manchester, Eng.: Manchester Univ. Press, 1984), 55–56. All subsequent references to this work appear in the text.

Introducing the B-Effect ❏

Jameson's and Eagleton's confusions before postmodern culture typify the prevalence of the unfortunate theoretical virus that one might best define as the *B-effect*; that is, the needlessly catastrophic sense of critical and creative crisis culled by lesser *bricoleurs,* such as Bürger, Bonita-Oliva, and Belsey, from the writings of such European sages and semisages as Benjamin, Brecht, Beckett, Barthes, Baudrillard, and Bourdieu. According to this mythology, all postmodern discourses, be they borrowed from past, present, or future, appear "doomed, doomed to fail,"[1] while every postmodern *penseur,* be that person a professor, poet, or punk, seems fated to perceive his or her present as a condition affording "no future" (to employ punk rhetoric) or "the loss in Post-modernism of the sense of the future" and "a sense that nothing will change and there is no hope" (to cite Jameson's formulation).[2]

Defined still more melodramatically, in Jean Baudrillard's address entitled "The Year 2000 Will Not Take Place," it would appear that "each fact, each political, historical, cultural act is endowed, by its power of media diffusion, with a kinetic energy which flings it out of its own space forever, and propels it into hyperspace where it loses all meaning, since it can never return."[3]

Having established that the kinetic energy of postmodern experience accelerates and annihilates historical meaning, Baudrillard further argues that the "silent power" of the masses' indifference simultaneously decelerates and neutralizes all sense of history. Accordingly,

7

history stops here, and we see in what way: not for want of people, nor of violence . . . nor of events . . . but by deceleration, indifference and stupefaction. History can no longer outrun itself, it can no longer envisage its own finality, dream of its own end; it is buried in its own immediate effect, it implodes in the here and now. Finally, we cannot even speak of the end of history, because *there is no time* for it to reach its own end. Its effects accelerate, but its progress ineluctably slows down. It will come to a standstill, and fade out like light and time on the edge on an infinitely dense mass.[4]

Notes

1. Samuel Beckett, *Watt*, (1953; rpt., London: John Calder, 1963), 61.
2. Jameson, *Flash Art*, 73.
3. Jean Baudrillard, "The Year 2000 Will Not Take Place," trans. Paul Foss and Paul Patton, in *Futur*Fall: Excursions into Post-Modernity*, ed. E.A. Grosz et al. (Sydney: Power Institute of Fine Arts, 1986), 19.
4. Baudrillard, "The Year 2000," 20–21.

Introducing the C-Effect ❑

At this point, it is salutary to reconsider the quite antithetical postmodern ethos and aesthetic of the American composer John Cage or what we may now identify as the *C-effect* in postmodern culture. Impressively immune to the hypotheses of the B-effect, the C-effect logic of Cage's writings insists upon the viability and the value of the variously conceptual and technological innovations that Lyotard defines as "new moves," "new rules," and "new games" (*Postmodern Condition*, 53).

Thus, whereas Baudrillard and Jameson associate the impact of postmodern architecture and of the postmodern mass media with the masses' "indifference" and "stupefaction" and with the intellectual's crises of representation and conceptualization, Cage argues that the architectural and technological innovations of postmodern culture permit potential global enlightenment and improvement and invite positive new modes of representation and conceptualization. In Cage's terms, "the media we use are effecting the metamorphosis of our minds and bringing us to our senses."[1]

As Cage explains in the introduction to *A Year from Monday*, the general tenor of his conclusions may well spring from his most "redeeming quality . . . a sunny disposition."[2] Yet Cage's conclusions are not so much the naive affirmations of an urban transcendentalist as the considered judgments of one of the most positively informed critics of contemporary culture. Whereas most theorists contributing to the B-effect appear so transfixed by the oversimplistic negative clichés of current cultural commentary that they genuinely believe that history, art, and meaning in general "stop here," Cage's awareness of, and insistence upon, the most positive and productive writings of his contemporaries leads him to champion those postmodern innovations that offer possibilities of "starting here" or "restarting here." Introducing his general philosophy, Cage explains,

At any point in time, there is a tendency when one "thinks" about world society to "think" that things are fixed, cannot change. This non-changeability is imaginary, invented by "thought" to simplify the process of "thinking." But thinking is nowadays complex. . . . Our minds are changing . . . to a courageous seeing of things in movement, life as revolution.[3]

Cage defines such courageous thinking in terms of the writings of the architect Buckminster Fuller, contending, "He more than any other to my knowledge sees the world situation—all of it—clearly and has fully reasoned projects for turning our attention away from 'killingry' toward 'livingry.' "[4] Summarizing Fuller's project as the aspiration "to triple the effectiveness and to implement the distribution of world resources so that everyone in the world will have what he needs," Cage concludes that social leadership must be "radical, global, architectural," adding, "architectural in the sense that Buckminster Fuller uses the word: comprehensive design problem-solving."[5]

As is so often the case in Cage's writings, Cage's positive and predominantly metaphorical deployment of a term finds quite antithetical counterparts in the writings of B-effect theory. So far as Baudrillard is concerned, postmodern architecture is synonymous not so much with Fuller's global projects as with the trivia of Parisian supermarkets. Identifying the underground shopping centers of Les Halles as quintessential icons of postmodernity, Baudrillard describes them as "the undergound sarcophagus" and the "museum of our culture" built by those who "already scent the terror of the year 2000" for the benefit of "future generations, after the catastrophe."[6] Jameson similarly interprets late modern and postmodern architecture as symptoms of terminal cultural decay. Apparently, the proliferation of shoddy "glass boxes in all the major urban centers in the world" testifies that "high modernism can be definitely certified as dead and as a thing of the past: its Utopian ambitions . . . unrealizable and its formal innovations exhausted."[7]

Notes

1. John Cage, *A Year from Monday* (1969; rpt., Middletown, Conn.: Wesleyan Univ. Press, 1979), 164.
2. Cage, *A Year from Monday*, x.
3. Cage, *A Year from Monday*, 166.
4. Cage, *A Year From Monday*, ix.
5. Cage, *A Year from Monday*, 165.
6. Baudrillard, "The Year 2000," 25.
7. Fredric Jameson, Foreword to *Postmodern Condition*, by Lyotard, xvii.

Deploring/Exploring Hyperspace: Jameson and Cage ❑

Jameson's thoughts on postmodern architecture are couched in Baudrillardian mumbo jumbo about "hyperspace," or "a situation where subjects and objects have been dissolved," and he somewhat eccentrically concludes,

> What is striking about the new urban ensembles around Paris and elsewhere in Europe is that there is *absolutely no perspec-*

tive at all. Not only has the street disappeared . . . but all profiles have disappeared as well. This is bewildering and I use existential bewilderment in this new postmodernist space to make a final diagnosis of the loss of our ability to *posit ourselves within this space and cognitively map it.* This is then projected back on the emergence of a global multinational culture which is decentered and cannot position itself.[1]

As one might anticipate, Cage's responses to such urban ensembles are far more optimistic. According to Cage, the omnipresence of glass-fronted, postmodernist space inaugurates the capacity to "see several things at once . . . as though we lived . . . in Rome where you see many centuries interpenetrating."[2] Jameson's confusions seem twofold. His initial incapacity to map new urban spaces with old cartographical concepts seems to aggravate his subsequent indisposition to contemplate new urban spaces in terms of new categories such as the concepts of reflection, collage, and transparency entertained by Cage. Introducing these concepts, Cage comments,

> I think that a great deal of our experience comes from the large use of glass in our architecture, so that our experience is one of reflection, collage, and transparency. I think these elements are very important and very different from a life that had less glass in it![3]

Cage concedes that such terms await definition, adding, "I don't think we know all the words yet that describe the effect on the other senses. I mean to say, we could accept the word 'collage' in music. 'Transparency' becomes a little more difficult, and 'reflection.' "[4] But his writings insist that the contemporary sensibility *may* potentially make sense of its environment. Even if we sense that "nowadays everything happens at once," Cage argues that "our souls are conveniently electronic (omniattentive),"[5] spiritual or cerebral tortoises, as it were, which are always potentially apace with, or ahead of, the hares of material, mechanical, and multinational change. Discussing the problems arising from the new technology, Cage posits that "we have a grand power that we're just becoming aware of in our minds," maintaining that we are—or should be—"dimly" aware that our minds are "in advance of the technology."[6]

Discussing his early work with radio, Cage admits that he has not always worked comfortably with postmodern technology but insists, nevertheless, that the postmodern sensibility may come to terms with technology by using it, studying it, and thereby *dehexing* it.

> My thinking was that I didn't like the radio and that I would be able to like it if I used it in my work. That's the same kind of thinking that we ascribe to the cave dwellers in their drawings of the frightening animals on the walls—that through making the pictures of them that they would come to terms with them. I did that later with the tape machine in Milan when I went to make *Fontana Mix*. I was alarmed over all the possibilities, so I simply sat down the first day I was there and drew a picture of the whole machine. That dehexed it for you, so to speak.[7]

Cage's equanimity offers an inspiring antidote to Jameson's apocalyptic pessimism. Whereas Jameson qualifies his suggestion that artists and theorists might perhaps explore new worlds with the assertion that the postmodern experience of "*intensities* of highs and lows" restricts one within "a kind of non-humanist experience of limits beyond which you get dissolved,"[8] Cage seems to envisage a more positive and more productive exploration of these limits, predicting greater awareness of the mind's "grand power," rather than its dissolution.

Accordingly, Cage rejects the limitations of the past rather than worrying about the limitations of the present and the future, and he advocates innovation and education rather than compliant complaint: "Our education has kept our minds stunted, and we are going to change that situation. Our minds are going to be stretched. We are going to stretch ourselves to the breaking point."[9]

Notes

1. Jameson, *Flash Art*, 70.
2. Cage, *Eyeline*, 6.
3. Cage, *Eyeline*, 6.
4. Cage, *Eyeline*, 7.

5. John Cage, letter to the *Village Voice*, 20 Jan. 1966, in *John Cage*, ed. Richard Kostelanetz (London: Allen Lane, 1971), 167.

6. John Cage, "Conversation with Richard Kostelanetz" (1968), in *John Cage*, 25.

7. John Cage and Richard Kostelanetz, "A Conversation about Radio in Twelve Parts" (manuscript, 1985), 21.

8. Jameson, *Flash Art*, 69.

9. Cage, "Conversation with Kostelanetz," in *John Cage*, 25.

Stupefaction or Enlivenment? ❏

Embracing and advocating the advantages of postmodernism's quintessentially technological discourses, Cage's correspondence of 1956 stirringly affirms, "Machines are here to stay, or for the time being. They can tend toward our stupefaction or our enlivenment. To me, the choice seems obvious, and once taken, cries for action."[1] Cage's refusal of the postmodern era's forces of stupefaction and his insistence upon the postmodern artist's capacity for enlivened action finds few resonances among the "B's" of postmodern theory or among such carriers of the B-effect as Eagleton and Jameson. While obvious parallels exist between Cage's theories and the manifestos of avant-garde European modernists such as the futurist Marinetti, who likewise envisaged the advantages of "man multiplied by the machine,"[2] the B-effect seems to nip postmodernism's mechanical discourses in the bud by diagnosing their futility in the bud, as though these media, like Beckettian humanity in *Waiting for Godot*, "give birth astride of a grave."[3] Not content with identifying the axiomatically inauthentic quality of postmodern culture as a whole, Eagleton further suggests that "postmodernism is among other things a sick joke at the expense of . . . revolutionary avant-gardism" ("Capitalism, Modernism," 60). It would be more accurate to argue that the misanthropic and myopic assumptions contributing to the B-effect proliferate sick jokes at the expense of the new ante-art of the modernist and postmodern avant-gardes.

While postmodern creativity as "a new cultural logic" (to quote one of Jameson's happier terms)[4] begs definition in terms of international referents, these pages will attempt to indicate the general parameters of this new cultural logic in predominantly transatlantic terms—not so much in any hope of charting the parameters of postmodernism as a whole as in the attempt to neutralize the myths generated by the B-effect by reference to the antithetical assumptions of those North American artists contributing in action, if not in initial, to the C-effect. By way of transition between these two groups, further consideration will be given to Jameson's ponderings upon contemporary American art. As will become apparent, the B-effect frequently misrepresents the most interesting suppositions of such "B's" of European theory and literature as Benjamin, Barthes, Beckett, and Baudrillard. Perhaps these pages will sporadically offer them slightly more justice.

Notes

1. John Cage, letter to Paul Henry Lang, 22 May 1956, in *John Cage*, 118.

2. F. T. Marinetti, "Destruction of Syntax-Imagination Without Strings-Words-in-Freedom" (1913), trans. R. W. Flint, in *Futurist Manifestos*, ed. Umbro Apollonio (London: Thames and Hudson, 1973), 97.

3. Samuel Beckett, *Waiting for Godot* (1956; rpt., London: Faber and Faber, 1977), 89.

4. Jameson, *Flash Art*, 69.

Benjamin and the Loss of Aura ☐

The B-effect (or at least, concepts contributing to the B-effect) may be traced to the very dawn of the postmodern era, in Walter Benjamin's celebrated essay, "The Work of Art in the Age of Mechanical Reproduction" (1936). Here, Benjamin misleadingly meditates upon the "decay" (225), the "shriveling" (233), and the "destruction" (240) of what he calls the "aura of art." Proposing that this aura, or the sense of a work's uniqueness, is "inseparable from its being imbedded in the fabric of tradition" (225), Benjamin suggests that "the technique of reproduction detaches the reproduced object from the domain of tradition" so that "that which withers in the age of mechanical reproduction is the aura of the work of art" (223). At best, Benjamin offers a half-truth.

Considered from the perspective of such early advocates of the C-effect as the futurist artist Carlo Carrà, those experimenting with new mechanical discourses could claim to be "the *primitives of a completely renovated sensitiveness*" and pioneers of a new, twentieth century tradition.[1] Cage's "History of Experimental Music in the United States" (1958), in *Silence*, makes much the same claim for the American sensibility.

> Actually America has an intellectual climate suitable for radical experimentation. We are, as Gertrude Stein said, the oldest country of the twentieth century. And I like to add: in our way of knowing newness. . . . Once in Amsterdam, a Dutch musician said to me, "It must be difficult for you in America to write music, for you are so far away from the centers of tradition." I had to say, "It must be difficult for you in Europe to write music, for you are so close to the centers of tradition."[2]

Benjamin more or less shares Carrà's and Cage's enthusiasms for radical experimentation and technological newness when he posits that a "changed technological standard" is the very precondition of "any new art form" (239), with—presumably—its own new aura and its own new tradition. But he is less helpful when he hints that technological creativity impoverishes art. Crude technological creativity, like crude pretechnological creativity, may well dismay the cultural critic. But this does not mean that mechanical culture axiomatically abolishes authentic art. Cage's address on "Experimental Music" surely carries more conviction when it proposes that "the coming into being of something new does not by that fact deprive what was of its proper place. Each thing has its proper place, never takes the place of something else; and the more things there are, as is said, the merrier" (*Silence*, 11).

Notes

1. Umberto Boccioni, Carlo Carrà, Luigi Russolo, Giacomo Balla, and Gino Severini, "The Exhibitors to the Public" (1912), trans. Caroline Tisdall, in *Futurist Manifestos*, 49.
2. John Cage, "History of Experimental Music in the United States" (1958), in *Silence* (1961; rpt., Middletown, Conn.: Wesleyan Univ. Press, 1983), 73. All subsequent references to Cage's writings refer to *Silence* unless otherwise indicated and appear in the text.

Barthes, Belsey, and the Death of the Author ❏

Most of the misconceptions contributing to the B-effect stem from the apocalyptic critic's refusal to countenance this pluralistic, "merrier" concept of culture. In one way or another, the B-effect hails or bewails the passing of this or that cultural tradition so that the history of postmodernism becomes a litany of extinction rather than a chronology of creation. Benjamin, as we have observed, starts the ball rolling by recording the "shriveling" of art's aura.

Barthes, in his turn, invented the "death of the author," announcing that "the text is henceforth made and read in such a way that at all its levels the author is absent,"[1] while post-Barthesian, poststructuralist zealots, such as Catherine Belsey, have been moved to proclaim, "The epoch of the metaphysics of presence is doomed, and with it all the methods of analysis, explanation and interpretation which rest on a single, unquestioned, pre-Copernican centre."[2]

This is very pretty, but it is surely taking Barthesian bluff too far, too fast, and too uncritically. Those who quote Barthes's beautifully ironic assertion that the writer may "only imitate a gesture that is always anterior, never original" and only "mix writings"[3] both imitate and invalidate these hypotheses, by asserting that the author, Barthes, very originally discerned the impossibility of authorial originality. Canonizing her master's voice, Belsey concludes that "in reality,"

> the author's subjectivity, itself constructed in language, is "only a ready-formed dictionary, its words only explainable through other words, and so on indefinitely." . . . Unable, therefore, to "express" a unique and transcendent subjectivity, the author in practice constructs a text by assembling intertextual fragments. (*Critical Practice*, 134)

In reality, as Barthes's later meditations more helpfully acknowledge, the assembling of intertextual fragments generates two distinct effects: the anonymous banality of those works that he deems reducible to the "ready-formed" conventions of *studium*; and the mystery of those irreducible traces of authorial aura, subjectivity, and originality that Barthes associates with the impact of photographic *punctum*.[4] Eventually, Barthes's theories challenge the misanthropy of the B-effect and confirm Marinetti's and Cage's confidence in the new media, somewhat as Samuel Beckett (an erstwhile pillar of the B-effect) experimented with television and regretted that it was too late for him to "go the whole hog" with new multimedia creativity.[5]

Notes

1. Roland Barthes, "The Death of the Author," in *Image-Music-Text*, 145.

2. Catherine Belsey, *Critical Practice* (London: Methuen, 1980), 137. All subsequent references to this work appear in the text.

3. Barthes, "Death of the Author," 146.

4. Roland Barthes, *Camera Lucida: Reflections on Photogra-*

phy, trans. Richard Howard (New York: Hill and Wang, 1981), 51.

5. Samuel Beckett expressed his regret that he could not "go the whole hog" with technology, in conversation with the author, 30 Jan. 1986.

Bürger and the Death of the Avant-Garde ❑

The other "B's" of European postmodernity are seldom so perceptive. According to Peter Bürger, the bewildering simultaneity of radically disparate contemporary techniques and styles makes it impossible for any "movement in the arts today" to "legitimately claim to be historically more advanced *as art* than any other."[1] In Bürger's terms, the pluralism of contemporary art practices along with the commercial success of these practices combine to neutralize authentic avant-garde innovation. Bürger concludes,

> To formulate more pointedly: the neo-avant-garde institutionalizes the *avant-garde as art* and thus negates genuinely avant-garde intentions. This is true independently of the consciousness artists have of their activity. . . . It is the status of their products, not the consciousness artists have of their activity, that defines the social effect of works. (*Theory of the Avant-Garde*, 58)

Bürger's conclusions pivot upon the limitations of his own particular concept of "genuine avant-garde intentions." Bürger perceives genuinely avant-garde work to be inseparable from social and institutional intent, insofar as it must make "a break with the traditional representational system" and must apparently effect "the total abolition of the institution that is art" (63). Perturbed to find that the postmodern avant-garde should coexist within the simultaneity of other contemporary representational systems and graver still, should seem content to function both as oddity and as commodity within the cultural and commercial "institution that is art," Bürger denies its exis-

18

tence as avant-garde experimentation. Observing that "the procedures invented by the avant-garde with antiartistic intent are being used for artistic ends," Bürger concludes that such modes of avant-garde art "lose their character as antiart" and become, in the museum, "an autonomous work among others" (57).

Bürger's distress seems to arise from his compulsion to define and confine postmodern avant-garde creativity within the narrow terms peculiar to the political, left-wing, segment of the modernist avant-garde. Put more figuratively, Bürger attempts not merely to put new wine into old bottles, but into *red* bottles at that. Arguably, the modernist avant-garde falls into at least three different variants of anti-artistic intent.

At its most negative point, the modernist avant-garde culminates in the anti-art of Marcel Duchamp, whose work, as Duchamp clearly explained, aspired neither to political nor aesthetic ideals but "was based on a reaction of *visual indifference* with a total absence of good or bad taste . . . in fact a complete anaesthesia."[2] Elsewhere, as Kurt Schwitters indicates in "Merz" (1920), modernist anti-art was created by those artists, like Schwitters, who aimed "only at art" (or who, in Bürger's terms, employed "antiartistic intent . . . for artistic ends"), and by those artists, like Huelsenbeck, who were exclusively "orientated towards politics."[3]

The postmodern avant-garde exhibits similar polarities. In this respect, Bürger's conclusions are impoverished both by their partisan assumption that avant-garde art should be ordered exclusively towards politics and by their anachronistic assumption that the postmodern avant-garde should abide by modernist avant-garde conventions.

At best, Bürger defines the postmodern avant-garde's practices negatively by delineating the ways in which they differ from the example of certain of their precursors. At worst, Bürger, like his fellow contributors to the B-effect, melodramatically misjudges the complex dynamics of postmodern culture by contorting its phases within what one might think of as the rhetoric of "the final solution."

Enthusiastically identifying the "conclusion" (22), the "com-

pleted evolution" (26), the "terminal point" (49), or the "abolition" (63) of this or that artistic or institutional tradition, Bürger's argument insists that avant-garde art must either break
with and abolish its parent institutions or else be broken with
and abolished by its critics and historians. Not surprisingly,
Bürger's *Theory of the Avant-Garde* exterminates its object.[4] So
far as Bürger is concerned, the postmodern era witnesses "the
end of the historical avant-garde movements" (liii).

Notes

1. Peter Bürger, *Theory of the Avant-Garde*, trans. Michael
Shaw (Manchester, Eng.: Manchester Univ. Press, 1984), 63. All
subsequent references to this work appear in the text.
2. Marcel Duchamp, qtd. by Hans Richter, in *Dada: Art and
Anti-Art*, trans. David Britt (1965; rpt., London: Thames and
Hudson, 1970), 89.
3. Kurt Schwitters, "Merz" (1920), trans. Ralph Mannheim,
in *Dada Painters and Poets*, ed. Robert Motherwell (1951; rpt.,
New York: George Wittenborn, 1967), 60.
4. Lyotard remarks upon the same kind of impulse in a
more general context, observing, "When power assumes the
name of a party, realism and its neoclassical complement tri-
umph over the experimental avant-garde by slandering it and
banning it" (*Postmodern Condition*, 75).

Bonito-Oliva, Baudrillard, and the
Collapse of the New ❑

One discovers much the same conclusions in the writings of
the Italian art historian and polemicist Achille Bonito-Oliva.
Conflating Bürger's thesis with both his own enthusiasm for
the revived expressionism of the Italian *trans-avant-garde* and
with the extravagant revelations of the French visionary Jean
Baudrillard, Bonito-Oliva boosts the B-effect by diagnosing the
death of the high-tech postmodern avant-garde. According to
Bonito-Oliva's reasoning, the superficiality of the contemporary

mass media "has caused the historical optimism of the avant-garde—the idea of progress inherent in its experimentation with new techniques and new materials—to collapse."[1]

The Nostradamus of postmodernism, Jean Baudrillard, draws attention to the still more apolcalyptic "liquidation of all referentials." Apparently, the contemporary mass media not only lack aura but mask, pervert, and *dissolve* reality into "its own pure simulacrum."[2] Like Benjamin and Barthes, Baudrillard makes best sense when he too acknowledges that for all their limitations, the new media also sometimes generate their own aura or *punctum*—or in Baudrillard's contagious terminology, their ambiguous "obscenity."[3]

Notes

1. Achille Bonita-Oliva, *Trans-avantgarde International*, trans. Dwight Gast and Gwen Jones (Milan: Giancarlo Politi Editore, 1982), 8. All subsequent references to this work appear in the text.

2. Jean Baudrillard, "The Precession of Simulacra," trans. Paul Foss and Paul Patton, in *Simulations* (New York: Semiotext(e), 1983), 11, 4.

3. Jean Baudrillard, "The Ecstasy of Communication," trans. John Johnston, in *The Anti-Aesthetic: Essays on Post-Modern Culture*, ed. Hal Foster (Port Townsend, Wash.: Bay, 1983), 130.

Beckett, Brecht, and the Attractions of Antinarrative □

Preparing the way, as it were, for Baudrillard's ever more seductive analyses of postmodernism's apotheosis, pioneer postmodern antinarrators such as Beckett and Brecht repudiated earlier modes of narrative and antinarrative. Both deride the realist rhetoric that Beckett evokes in terms of "clockwork cabbages . . . staying put wherever needed"[1] and that Brecht associates with conventional modes of "growth" and "linear development."[2] Likewise, both reject the symbolist antirhetoric that Beckett equates with the harmonious "indirect and comparative" observations of modernists such as Proust.[3]

Evincing neither the realist's "plausible concatenation" nor the modernist's "transcendental aperception," Beckett's and Brecht's antinarratives precipitate peculiarly *unharmonious* evocations of existence, bequeathing the Beckettian challenge, "Make sense who may," or the Brechtian protest, "That's extraordinary, hardly believable."[4] The contrasting implications of the Beckettian challenge and the Brechtian protest epitomize the bifurcation between the political and apolitical modes of early European postmodern antinarrative. As the examples from Beckett's and Brecht's poetry in the following section indicate, Beckett's antinarratives respond primarily to his sense of the inadequacy of language and the anguish of survival and self-knowledge, whereas Brechtian antinarrative tends to address wider social and ideological issues, such as the "great man" theory of history. Considered from the European perspective, postmodern antinarrative is usually misinterpreted from either an excessively Beckettian perspective or an excessively Brechtian perspective.

Transfixed by Beckett's provocative avowal that "to be an artist is to fail as no other dare fail,"[5] Beckettian devotees tend to caricature postmodern literature in terms of a hypothetically pervasive "poetics of failure," "art of failure," "logic of failure," or "fidelity to failure."[6] Equally misleading Brechtian readings of postmodern writings convince critics such as Catherine Belsey that most responses to expressive realism are interrogative attempts to "write a new kind of text, foregrounding contradiction" in the Brechtian manner, thereby "distancing the audience from both text and ideology" (*Critical Practice*, 128). As becomes evident, these predominantly European variants of postmodern creativity beg comparison with a third, predominantly North American mode of antinarrative peculiar to the work of multimedia postmoderns such as John Cage, Laurie Anderson, Philip Glass, and Robert Wilson.

Notes

1. Samuel Beckett condemns Balzac's characters as "clockwork cabbages" in his first novel, the unpublished "Dream of Fair to Middling Women," 1932, Beckett Collection, 1227/7/16/8:106, Reading Univ. Collection.

2. Bertolt Brecht contrasts conventional narrative growth and linear development with the strategies of his Epic Theatre in "Notes on Opera" (1930), in *Brecht on Theatre*, trans. and ed. John Willett (1964; rpt., New York: Hill and Wang, 1977), 37.

3. Samuel Beckett, *Proust* (1931), rpt. as *Proust and Three Dialogues with Georges Duthuit* (London: John Calder, 1970), 88. As Beckett observes, Proust's "indirect and comparative" observations are reconciled within "the chain-figure of the metaphor" (88). (I discuss the antimetaphorical impulse in postmodern fiction in "Postmodernity, *Métaphore manquée*, and the Myth of the Trans-avant-garde," *SubStance*, 14.3 (1986): 68–90).

4. The reference to the realist's "plausible concatenation" and the modernist's "transcendental aperception" can be found in Beckett, *Proust and Three Dialogues*, 82, 90. The Beckettian challenge is found in Samuel Beckett, *What Where* (1983), in *Collected Shorter Plays* (London: Faber and Faber, 1984), 316. The Brechtian protest appears in Bertolt Brecht, "Theatre for Pleasure or Theatre for Instruction" (ca. 1936), in *Brecht on Theatre*, 71.

5. Beckett, *Proust and Three Dialogues*, 125.

6. Michael Robinson refers to Beckett's "poetics of failure" in *The Long Sonata of the Dead: A Study of Samuel Beckett* (Edinburgh: Oliver and Boyd, 1964), 4; and Leo Bersani alludes to Beckett's logic of failure and fidelity to failure in *Balzac to Beckett: Center and Circumference in French Fiction* (New York: Oxford Univ. Press, 1970), 317.

Beckett's Poetics of Failure/Brecht's Poetics of Interrogation ❑

It is easy to understand why postmodern antinarrative should initially have seemed inseparable from a Beckettian "poetics of failure." As the following lines from the addenda to Beckett's

Watt suggest, language seems incapable of containing or conveying the painful experience of age, absence, suffering, and nothingness:

> who may tell the tale
> of the old man?
> weigh suffering in a scale?
> mete want with a span?
> the sum assess
> of the world's woes?
> nothingness
> in words enclose?[1]

Brecht's poem "A Worker Reads, and Asks These Questions" is obviously motivated by quite different considerations, despite its similarly interrogative format.

> Who built Thebes with its seven gates?
> In all the books it says kings.
> Did kings drag up those rocks from the quarry?
> And Babylon, overthrown time after time,
> Who built it up as often? . . .

> The Young Alexander took India.
> By himself?
> Caesar hammered Gaul.
> Had he not even a cook beside him? . . .

> Someone wins on every page.
> Who cooked the winners' banquet?
> One great man every ten years.
> Who paid the expenses?

> So many statements.
> So many questions.[2]

As Brecht specifies in "Theatre for Pleasure or Theatre for Instruction" (ca. 1936), his readers and audiences are invited to react by responding, "That's not the way," or "It's got to stop."[3] While Brecht's later writings, such as his *A Short Organum for the Theatre* (1948), modify his intent to the extent of postulating that it is the business of the theater "to entertain people" and "to remain something entirely superfluous,"[4] his poetry and drama fit comfortably into neither of these categories. On the contrary, Brechtian antinarrative purposefully

24

generates questions in search of answers and problems in search of practical solutions. "On the Use of Music in an Epic Theatre" (1935) explains,

> The concern of the epic theatre is . . . eminently practical. Human behaviour is shown as alterable; man himself as dependent on certain political and economic factors and at the same time as capable of altering them. To give an example: a scene where three men are hired by a fourth for a specific illegal purpose (*Mann ist Mann*) has to be shown by the epic theatre in such a way that it becomes possible to imagine the attitude of the four men other than as it is expressed there: i.e., so that one imagines either a different set of political and economic conditions under which these men would be speaking differently, or else a different approach on their part to their actual conditions, which would likewise lead them to say different things.[5]

Accordingly,

> the spectator is given the chance to criticize human behaviour from a point of view, and the scene is played as a piece of history. The idea is that the spectator should be put in a position where he can make comparisons about everything that influences the way in which human beings behave.

Beckett pointedly denies such didactic intent. Discussing the general impact of *Endgame,* he tellingly insists, "We have no elucidations to offer. . . . My work is a matter of fundamental sounds . . . made as fully as possible, and I accept responsibility for nothing else. If people want to have headaches among the overtones, let them. And provide their own aspirin."[6] Central here seems to be Beckett's emphasis upon his incapacity to accept responsibility for anything other than an authentic demonstration of "fundamental sounds . . . made as fully as possible" (a confession that the Lukácsian reader would doubtless dismiss as further evidence of Beckett's incapacity to evoke anything other than images of "the utmost human degradation").[7]

Yet while Beckett's modest proposal offers neither the Lukácsian ideal of "a sense of *perspective*" (*Meaning of Contemporary Realism*, 33) nor the Brechtian ambition to make the spectator "criticize human behaviour," Beckett's writings share the same high seriousness. Whether Beckett addresses the positive "time-honoured conception of humanity in ruins," which he associated with the solidarity of those working in the Red Cross Hospital at Saint-Lô in 1946; the *mess* and the *distress* evoked by his postwar fiction; or the ghostly *comfort* depicted in his most recent plays for stage and television, he seems consistently concerned with fundamental experience.[8]

Notes

1. Beckett, *Watt*, 247.

2. Bertolt Brecht, "A Worker Reads, and Asks These Questions," in *Rites of Passage*, trans. Edwin Morgan (Manchester: Carcanet, 1976), 143.

3. Brecht, "Theatre for Pleasure or Theatre for Instruction," 71.

4. Bertolt Brecht, *A Short Organum for the Theatre* (1948), in *Brecht on Theatre*, 180, 181.

5. Bertolt Brecht, "On the Use of Music in an Epic Theatre" (1935), in *Brecht on Theatre*, 86.

6. Samuel Beckett, letter to Alan Schneider , 2 Dec. 1957, in *Disjecta: Miscellaneous Writings and a Dramatic Fragment by Samuel Beckett*, ed. Ruby Cohn (London: John Calder, 1983), 109.

7. Georg Lukács, *The Meaning of Contemporary Realism*, trans. John and Necke Mander (1963; rpt., London: Merlin, 1972), 31.

8. Beckett discusses the positive "time honoured conception of humanity in ruins" in "The Capital of the Ruins," a radio script (1946), in *As No Other Dare Fail* (London: John Calder, 1986),75–76. Beckett's allusions to the "mess" and the "distress" of existence appear in Tom F. Driver's article "Beckett by the Madeleine," *Columbia University Forum* 4 (Summer 1961): 21, 22. Beckett evokes the comfort sent by a departed "dear name" in *Ohio Impromptu* and the compassionate ministerings of hands sent from "a kinder light" in *Nacht und Träume*, both in *Collected Shorter Plays*, 287, 305.

Beckett, Brecht, and the Groan of the Text ❑

Without wishing to belittle either Brecht's or Beckett's achievements with the levity of alliterative antitheses, one might posit that whereas Brecht's and Beckett's respective evocations of fundamental sounds activate what one might think of as the *groan of the text*, American modes of postmodern antinarrative frequently approximate far more closely the superficial entertainment that Brecht's later writings associate with the theater[1] and might be characterized as modes of predominantly whimsical antinarrative eliciting the *grin of the text*.

This general distinction between antinarrative generating the *groan* of the text and antinarrative generating the *grin* of the text becomes evident when one contrasts Beckett's poetics of failure with the assumptions of such American postmodern poetics as the essays in John Cage's *Silence* (1961) or in Andy Warhol's *From A to B and Back Again* (1975). European and American responses to the postmodern condition are frequently significantly different in temper.

Note

1. Brecht, *A Short Organum for the Theatre*, 181.

Warhol and the Grin of the Text ❑

On many occasions, Beckett, Cage, and Warhol refer to the same general problems and employ remarkably similar concepts. Paradoxically, the causes of Beckett's *groan* frequently provide the catalyst for Cage's or Warhol's *grin*. For example, somewhat as Beckett insists that he cannot take responsibility for his audience's reactions to works such as *Endgame*, Warhol confides his unwillingness to accept any form of responsibility that might make him "miserable for years": "Sometimes people let the same problem make them miserable for years when they could just say, 'So what.' That's one of my favourite things to say. 'So what.' "[1] But whereas Beckett confesses to his irresponsibility with considerable sobriety, poignancy and—for lack of a better word—with considerable *responsibility*, attributing his failings to the trauma of "the day I became aware of my stupidity,"[2] Warhol complacently explains his irresponsibility away, musing, "I think I'm missing some chemicals and that's why I have this tendency to be more of—a mama's boy. A—sissy. No, a mama's boy. . . . I think I'm missing some responsibility chemicals" (*From A to B*, 105). In much the same way, Beckett's regret that his "people are falling to bits" and his confession that his work is dedicated to "that whole zone of being that has always been set aside by artists as something unusable—as something by definition incompatible with art"[3] find their relaxed counterpart in Warhol's nonchalant observation:

> "I always like to work on leftovers. . . . Things that were discarded, that everybody knew were no good, I always thought had a great potential to be funny. . . . I always thought there was a lot of humor in leftovers" (88).

Exemplifying what he means by the humor of such leftovers, Warhol resumes, "The other day I was on the Bowery and a person in a flophouse jumped out of the window and died, and a crowd went around the body, and then a bum staggered over and said, 'Did you see the comedy across the street?' " (106). Clearly a little embarrassed by his indifference to the pathos of this incident and by his bemusement before such "comedy," Warhol concludes,

> I'm not saying you have to be happy when a person dies, but just that it's curious to see cases where you don't *have* to be sad about it. . . . Remember though, that I think I'm missing some chemicals, so it's easier for me than a person who has a lot of responsibility chemicals. (106)

Notes

1. Andy Warhol, *From A to B and Back Again: The Philosophy of Andy Warhol* (1975; rpt., London: Picador, 1976), 105. All subsequent references to this work appear in the text.

2. Samuel Beckett, qtd. in *Samuel Beckett: A Biography*, by Deirdre Bair (London: Jonathan Cape, 1978), 367.

3. Samuel Beckett, qtd. in "Moody Man of Letters," by Israel Shenker, *New York Times*, 6 May, 1956, sec. 2, 3.

Eagleton, Jameson, and Dehistoricized Culture ❑

The self-consciously "very light, cool, off-hand, very American" (*From A to B*, 105) insouciance of Warhol's painting and prose frequently brings the B-effect to instant boiling point. Somewhat as Hitler condemned cubism, dadaism, futurism, and impressionism outright as the "artificious stammerings of men to whom God has denied the grace of a truly artistic talent, and in its place has awarded them with the gift of jabbering or deception,"[1] Eagleton's initial responses to postmodern culture dismiss it as bereft of "authenticity" and as "depthless, styleless, dehistoricized" ("Capitalism, Modernism," 61). Jameson likewise dismisses it as "speech in a dead language," evincing "a new kind of flatness or depthlessness" and "a new kind of superficiality in the most literal sense."[2] Arguing that Warhol "does not speak to us at all," Jameson contrasts such "great Warhol figures" as Marilyn Monroe with Munch's *The Scream* and introduces the "more general historical hypotheses" that "concepts such as anxiety and alienation [and the experiences to which they correspond, as in *The Scream*] are no longer appropriate in the world of the postmodern."[3]

Obvious exceptions to Jameson's hypothesis spring to mind. The English actress Billie Whitelaw, for example, describes her persona in Beckett's *Footfalls* precisely in terms of a "walking-talking Edvard Munch,"[4] hinting thereby that Beckett's postmodernism, at the very least, explores and refines dimensions of anxiety and alienation akin to that evoked by Munch. And as the following newspaper report of July 1986 testifies, one of Warhol's figures coincides almost exactly with Munch's *Scream*, provocatively problematizing authoriality, aesthetics, copyright, consumer values, and other aspects of the "unaccustomed new dilemmas in the areas of cultural production and theoretical understanding" that Jameson considers fundamental to the "institutional analysis" of postmodern culture.[5] The cultural gossip columnist of the *Weekend Australian* reports,

> Famed American painter Andy Warhol is in the soup . . . his work on Edvard Munch's *The Scream* (1893) . . . is bringing howls of anguish. According to well-informed London sources the Munch museum in Oslo is preparing legal action for breach of copyright. The Norwegians claim that although Warhol has reproduced the original *Scream* in every detail, changing nothing but the colours, he has not only signed his own name to it, but collects around $20,000 annually in copyright fees. The question is . . . is it still a Munch?[6]

Once one examines postmodern culture in terms of its varied practices, rather than in terms of the clichés of the B-effect, it becomes apparent that these practices are far more complex than Eagleton and Jameson initially assumed. Somewhat belatedly, Jameson's interview of December 1986 in *Flash Art* hesitantly adumbrated hypotheses that John Cage introduced nearly twenty years earlier, in an interview with Richard Kostelanetz (1968), in which he predicted that "our minds are going to be stretched . . . to the breaking point" in order to master new techniques and new technologies.[7] At his own pace, and in his own time, Jameson concedes that "some positive features of Postmodernism" may indeed employ the materials and media of commodification and "attempt somehow to master these things by choosing them and pushing them to their limits."[8]

Notes

1. Adolf Hitler, speech inaugurating the "Great Exhibition of German Art 1937," trans. Ilse Falk, in *Theories of Modern Art: A Source Book by Artists and Critics*, ed. Herschel B. Chipp (Berkeley: Univ. of California Press, 1968), 479.
2. Jameson, "Postmodernism, or the Cultural Logic," 65, 60.
3. Jameson, "Postmodernism, or the Cultural Logic," 59, 61.
4. Billie Whitelaw, qtd. in "Interview with Billie Whitelaw,"

by author, *Review of Contemporary Fiction* 7.2 (Summer 1987): 109.

5. Jameson, "Hans Haacke," 38.
6. *Weekend Australian Magazine*, 19–20 July 1986, 12.
7. Cage, "Conversation with Kostelanetz," in *John Cage*, 25.
8. Jameson, *Flash Art*, 72.

Cage, Kostelanetz, and Value Judgments ❑

In his 1968 interview with Richard Kostelanetz, Cage also suggests that it may be too soon to evaluate many postmodern experiments, insofar as their new discourses may neither respect nor prove susceptible to earlier aesthetic standards. Asked by Kostelanetz if some experimental theater pieces were "better than others," Cage rather disparagingly replied,

> Why do you waste your time and mine by trying to get value judgments? Don't you see that when you get a value judgment, that's all you have? They are destructive to our proper business, which is curiosity and awareness. . . . We must exercise our time positively. When I make these criticisms of other people, I'm not doing my own work; also, the people and their work may be changing.[1]

Cage memorably concludes, "The big thing to do actually is to get yourself into a situation that you use your experience in, even if you are at a performance of a work of art which, were you to criticize it, you would criticize it out of existence."

As Eagleton, Jameson, and the battalion of B-effect theorists and critics demonstrate, it is all too easy to criticize postmodern culture out of existence, be this by denying that it has *any* authenticity or that it has *anything* to say (as Eagleton and Jameson assert in their essays of the early eighties) or by suggesting that postmodernism is incompatible with "permanence and monumentality" (as Jameson still asserts in the late eighties). Significantly, Jameson now seems to share Cage's general suspicion of value judgments, which obscure attention to the "changing" existence of new creativity. Remarking that his

31

present ponderings upon postmodernity supersede their negative origins, Jameson explains,

> Since our first concepts of Postmodernism have tended to be negative (i.e. it isn't this, it isn't that, it isn't a whole series of things that Modernism was) ... the object is ultimately a positive description, not in any sense of value (so that Postmodernism would then "better" Modernism) but in order to grasp Postmodernism as a new cultural logic in its own right.[2]

Jameson's stubborn refusal to evaluate postmodern work differs significantly from Cage's rejection of premature and ill-informed value judgments. Maintaining the B-effect myth that postmodernity is somehow incompatible with aesthetic value, Jameson argues that the very essence of the postmodern work—and by extension, the very essence of one's experience of postmodern work—is a provisional *frisson* rather than anything more permanent or substantial, observing, "In dealing with Postmodernism, one can isolate people who made some pioneering contributions but aesthetic questions about how great these are—questions that can legitimately be posed when you're dealing with Modernism—make little sense."[3]

By contrast, Cage's criticism of his own work tends to confirm Lyotard's contention that postmodern work may indeed prove susceptible to aesthetic discrimination once one has discovered such works' implicit rules and aesthetic assumptions. According to Lyotard, in *The Postmodern Condition*,

> A postmodern artist or writer is in the position of a philosopher: the text he writes, the work he produces are not in principle governed by preestablished rules, and they cannot be judged according to a determining judgment, by applying familiar categories to the text or to the work. Those rules and categories are what the work of art itself is looking for. The artist and writer, then, are working without rules in order to formulate the rules of what *will have been done*. Hence the fact that work and text have the characters of an *event*. (81)

Notes

1. Cage, "Conversation with Kostelanetz," in *John Cage*, 27–28.

2. Jameson, *Flash Art*, 69.
3. Jameson, *Flash Art*, 72.

Jameson, Rauschenberg, and Premature Exasperation ❏

As his 1986 interview with Stephanson intimates, Jameson suffers from premature exasperation. Upon contemplating Rauschenberg's work, for example, he decrees it an event fated to be permanently *over* and therefore beyond aesthetic redemption because, by impatient Jamesonian logic, "all kinds of postmodernist experiences" are fated to be over, and so on. Jameson confusedly recounts,

> I don't know how great Rauschenberg is, but I saw a wonderful show of his in China, a glittering set of things which offered all kinds of postmodernist experiences. But when they're over, they're over. The textual object is not, in other words, a work of art, a "masterwork" like the Modernist monument was. You go into a Rauschenberg show and experience a process done in very expert and inventive ways; and when you leave, it's over.[1]

One wonders why the experience of reading Rauschenberg's work should become definitively *over* in this way. Perhaps the reader unfamiliar with Jameson's writings might damn them with similarly faint praise by dismissing them as a fleeting array of wonderful, postmodernist experiences, very expert and very inventive in their way, yet somehow unworthy of qualitative analysis.

Making reference to his enthusiasm for the teachings of Zen, Cage rather more positively asserts, "If something is boring after two minutes, try it for four. If still boring, try it for eight, sixteen, thirty-two, and so on. Eventually one discovers that it's not boring at all but very interesting" (*Silence*, 93). In other words, one suspects that Jameson's meditations upon Rauschenberg are overly hasty and could well have been ex-

tended beyond that point at which they seemed to be *over*, into
the realm of the *very interesting*.

Note

1. Jameson, *Flash Art*, 72.

Cage, Rauschenberg, and Ryman ❑

Contemplating Rauschenberg's work some quarter century
prior to Jameson's diagnosis of its apparent impermanence,
Cage's essay "On Robert Rauschenberg, Artist, and His Work"
(1961) admits that the conservative spectator might prefer more
traditional iconography (such as the gastronomic montages fa-
vored by the Dickensian diner). But he adds that the implications and connotations of Rauschenberg's works seem as varied
and as accessible as those of any earlier artist, once one accepts
their new rhetoric. "Would we have preferred a pig with an
apple in its mouth? That too, on occasion, is a message and
requires a blessing. These are the feelings Rauschenberg gives
us: love, wonder, laughter, heroism . . . fear, sorrow, anger,
disgust, tranquillity" (*Silence*, 101).

More recently, Cage has similarly insisted upon the inspira-
tional quality of Robert Ryman's white paintings. Whereas
Jameson dismisses unfamiliar art as something impermanent,
inconsequential, and inaccessible, Cage argues that the very
unfamiliarity of Ryman's work constitutes a catalyst for further
creativity. Discussing the experience of discovering Ryman's
work, Cage comments:

> The work of Ryman I was not familiar with, until I saw this
> retrospective show. And it was amazing to see what had hap-
> pened to his dedication to white. . . . The different materials
> on which he puts white, and the different ways in which he
> does it, are just extraordinary. And I came away from that
> exhibition with a renewed sense of joy, and even a joy close to
> a change of mind . . . the discoveries don't give you a loss of the

ability to discover, but rather, an intensification of that. . . . So that it's not just something becoming known, or increasing the known—it increases the unknown at the same time![1]

This is not to suggest that Cage's theories offer unconditional enthusiasm for the unknown or lack all sense of aesthetic judgment. On the contrary, Cage defines his own creative standards in terms of his intent "to sober and quiet the mind" and "to make sure that everything holds together."[2] Significantly, he criticizes compositions such as his *Alphabet* (1982) on the grounds that they prove "difficult to listen to" and are alternately "too simple" and "too complex."[3] Indeed, Cage introduces something approximating to an aesthetic of functionality when suggesting that experimental art should contribute to "the new ethic or new morality or new aesthetic."[4] Employing the rather ambiguous notion of *consumption*, Cage postulates, "We are having art in order to use it. Those things that we used have been consumed. We have to have fresh food now. You wouldn't ask me in the case of a steak I ate ten years ago somehow to regurgitate it and eat it over again, would you?"[5]

Notes

1. John Cage, interview with author, Geneva, 12 Sept. 1990.
2. Cage and Kostelanetz, "A Conversation about Radio," 32, 27.
3. Cage and Kostelanetz, "A Conversation about Radio," 30, 32.
4. Cage, "Conversation with Kostelanetz," in *John Cage*, 28.
5. Cage, "Conversation with Kostelanetz," in *John Cage*, 24.

Cage and Consumption ❑

Cage's concept of consumption is unusually positive, insofar as its notion of art "going right through the body and so forth," being consumed, and then leaving the need for something new constitutes an appeal for aesthetic progress. Rather than bewailing either the "effacement . . . of the older (essentially high-modernist) frontier between high culture and so-called mass or commercial culture" that Jameson discerns within postmodern culture or the "reification of everyday life in the capitalist marketplace" that Eagleton contrasts with the modernist reification of "the art work as isolated fetish" ("Capitalism, Modernism," 68), Cage advocates the avant-garde innovations that he associates with "freshness and newness and change."[1]

Appalled by consumer society in general, and by the particular ways in which "American, postmodern culture is the internal and superstructural expression of a whole wave of American military and economic domination throughout the world," Jameson initially condemns any and every mode of postmodern culture that seems tainted by the "forms, categories and contents of that very Culture Industry so passionately denounced by all the ideologues of the modern." More specifically, he deplores the use of "materials they no longer simply 'quote,' as a Joyce or a Mahler might have done, but incorporate into their very substance."[2] This is an odd hypothesis. The degraded, or notionally degraded, materials to which Jameson refers are incorporated into the works of all the key ideologues of modernist art, be these the collages, montages, and assemblages of the cubists, the expressionists, the futurists (Italian and Russian), the dadaists, the surrealists, or the constructivists.

Indeed, it is precisely because modernists like the pioneer collagist Kurt Schwitters argued that "old tickets, driftwood, cloak-room tabs, wires and wheel parts, buttons and old rubbish found in the attic and in rubbish dumps" could all prove "a material for painting just as good as the colours made in factories" and defended "freedom from all fetters, for the sake of artistic creation" that postmodernist artists such as Rauschenberg feel free to technologically and conceptually extend and modify the tradition of working with the *excess* of consumer society.[3]

Intimating that any honest postmodern work should incorporate every facet of postmodern culture, warts and all, Rauschenberg explains, "I was bombarded with TV sets and magazines . . . by the refuse, by the excess of the world. . . . I thought that if I could paint or make an honest work, it should incorporate all of these elements, which were and are a reality."[4]

Notes

1. Cage, "Conversation with Kostelanetz," in *John Cage*, 24. Jameson, "Postmodernism, or the Cultural Logic," 54.
2. Jameson, "Postmodernism, or the Cultural Logic," 57, 55.
3. Kurt Schwitters's argument for the various aesthetic materials is found in *Art International*, 25 Sept. 1960, 58. His defense of artistic freedom appears in "Merz," 59.
4. Robert Rauschenberg, qtd. in *The Shock of the New: Art and the Century of Change*, by Robert Hughes (London: British Broadcasting Corporation, 1980), 345.

Collective Narrative and the Struggle with Simulacra ❑

Despite his initial hostility to the use of the *refuse* of postmodernism's "whole 'degraded' landscape of schlock and kitsch," Jameson's admiration for the satirical political montages of the artist Hans Haacke now appears to persuade him that the subversive artist may "struggle within the world of the simulacrum by using the arms and weapons specific to that world which are themselves very precisely simulacra."[1] In a sense, of course, this is exactly what Rauschenberg and a whole generation of subsequent deconstructive artists have consistently achieved. Musing upon the way in which "people are made of images" (or at least conditioned by images), the novelist William Burroughs praises his fellow writer J. G. Ballard's *Love and Napalm: Export U.S.A.* (1972) precisely in terms of its exploration of such conditioning, asserting, "This is what Bob Rauschenberg is doing in art—literally blowing up the image."[2]

As their associate, the poet John Giorno, puts it, Rauschenberg and Warhol are "totally great" in terms of the way in which their provocative manipulation of consumer iconography "opened up American consciousness" and "cut through conceptualization."[3] Eloquently—and belatedly—defined by Jameson as the neutralization of reification "by means of reification in terms of reification," this subversive postmodern strategy is in

37

turn associated by Jameson with a predominantly detached, predominantly collective, "certain form of depersonalization"; a concept that seems to parallel Warhol's sense of his "very light, cool, off-hand" register or Rauschenberg's sense of his own similarly impersonal style.[4]

Here, as elsewhere, however, Jameson seems reluctant to acknowledge that such rhetoric is either particularly positive or particularly American. Instead, he rather ambiguously hints that its depersonalization derives from ideologically sounder *third world models*, or what he terms

> a third possibility beyond the old bourgeois self and the schizo-phrenic subject of our organization in society today: a *collective* subject, decentred but not schizophrenic. It emerges in certain forms of storytelling that can be found in Third World litera-ture, in testimonial literature, in gossip and rumours and things of this kind. It is storytelling which is neither personal in the modernist sense, nor depersonalized in the pathological sense of the schizophrenic text. It is decentred for the stories you tell . . . as an individual subject doesn't belong to you since you doesn't control them the way the master subject of Modernism would.[5]

A wide range of postmodern artists seem to associate the most positive forms of contemporary creativity with precisely this kind of *third possibility* beyond our organization in society today. But as the East German writer Heiner Müller indicates in the following aside from an interview with Sylvère Lotringer in 1988, European and American variants of this third possibil-ity are frequently extremely different: "Collective experience is not easy to define. Let's bring another bottle of whiskey, it will make it easier. . . . This is a serious problem and we should give ourselves time to address it."[6]

Notes

1. Jameson, in "Postmodernism, or the Cultural Logic," dis-cusses the "refuse" of postmodernism, 55. His discussion of sim-ulacra occurs in "Hans Haacke," 42–43.
2. William Burroughs, Introduction to *Love and Napalm: Ex-port U.S.A.*, by J. G. Ballard (New York: Grove, 1972), 7–8.

3. John Giorno, interview with Winston Leyland, *Gay Sunshine Interviews*, ed. Leyland (San Francisco: Gay Sunshine, 1978), 1:157.
4. Jameson, *Flash Art*, 72, 70–71. Rauschenberg discusses his impersonal style in Hughes's *The Shock of the New*, 345.
5. Jameson, *Flash Art*, 70–71.
6. Heiner Müller, "Wars," interview with Sylvère Lotringer (1988), in *Germania*, by Müller, ed. Lotringer, trans. Bernard and Caroline Schütze (New York: Semiotext(e), 1990), 76. All subsequent references to *Germania* appear in the text.

Depersonalized Culture or Repersonalized Culture? ❑

As will become evident, postmodern modes of collective art vary from high-tech, multimedia experiments to semishamanistic ritual. Jameson, for his part, insists that this third substantially impersonal and collective mode of postmodern narrative inaugurates nothing new. *"None of this,"* Jameson claims, *"is to invent style in the older sense"* (emphasis added).[1] Arguably, this third mode of narrative is far more innovative and far more individual than Jameson cares to concede. "Zero-degree" modes of collective postmodern culture may well eradicate individual accent—one thinks, for example, of disco music with its minimal lyrics and maximal, mechanical percussion. But the most interesting postmodern multimedia performers, particularly those that we have associated with the C-effect and with the grin of the text, combine both personal and impersonal materials in works that *depersonalize* content (by masking accent within variants of meter) and *repersonalize* content (by retaining and revealing sufficient accent to establish the singularity of both narrator and narrative material).

It is certainly true that postmodern narrators do not control their stories "the way that the master subject of Modernism would." But they *do* nevertheless control their stories the way that the master subject of postmodernism would by orchestrating materials according to modes of rule and chance and by depersonalizing or repersonalizing the content of their stories, by obscuring or by foregrounding variously live, technological, and live technological traces of authorial accent.

Barthes's essay entitled "The Grain of the Voice" (1972) associates this kind of authorial presence with vocal qualities existing "outside of any law"; Kristeva's meditations upon Barthes likewise testify to the "uncontourable" Barthesian accent that Kristeva identifies "in the fabric of sound" and as "beyond all signification"; while the American poet and artist Brion Gysin argues that despite the impersonality of Burrough's cut-up narratives, one need only take "one sniff of that prose," and "you'd say, 'Why, that's a Burroughs.' "[2] In much the same way, Cage's fellow composer Christian Wolff insists upon the individuality and the innovation of Cage's notionally impersonal compositions, observing, "His music . . . is like no other. I know of hardly anything that sounds like it."[3] Briefly, the subject is alive and well in postmodern culture, if often a little more fragmented than hitherto and frequently rather more *electronic* in character than its modernist precursors.

Whereas many of the most interesting modes of European postmodern creativity harken back to premodernist narrative modes, the peculiarly innovative quality of American postmodern performance may perhaps best be defined as the precipitate of curiously familiar and curiously unfamiliar narrative techniques imbued with the live or mechanically orchestrated grain or accent of the storyteller's voice. This kind of partially personal, partially impersonal, and partially collective mode of performance is typified by John Cage's *Indeterminacy* (1959).[4]

Randomly juxtaposing musical and electronic accompaniment, orchestrated by the musician David Tudor, alongside Cage's variously slow and variously rapid readings of a series of randomly ordered tales, *Indeterminacy* treats the listener to the following kind of ambulating and slightly inconclusive anecdote:

> When Xenia and I came to New York, we arrived in the bus station with about twenty-five cents. We were expecting to

stay for a while with Peggy Guggenheim and Max Ernst. Max Ernst had met us in Chicago and had said, "Whenever you come to New York, come and stay with us. We have a big house on the East River." I went to the phone booth in the bus station, put in a nickel, and dialed. Max Ernst answered. He didn't recognize my voice. Finally he said, "Are you thirsty." I said, "Yes." He said, "Well come over tomorrow for cocktails." I went back to Xenia and told her what had happened. She said, "Call him back. We have nothing to lose." I did. He said, "Oh! It's you. We've been waiting for you for weeks. Your room's ready. Come right over." (*Silence*, 12)

Notes

1. Jameson, *Flash Art*, 71.

2. Roland Barthes, "The Grain of the Voice" (1972), in *Image-Music-Text*, 188. Julia Kristeva, "La voix de Barthes," *Communications*, no. 36 (1982): 119. Kristeva refers to qualities "dans l'étoffe du son" and describes them as "incontourable" and as "avant la signification et au-delà d'elle." Brion Gysin discusses the inimitable quality of Burroughs's cut-ups in *Here to Go: Planet R-101*, by Terry Wilson and Brion Gysin (San Francisco: Re/Search, 1982), 191.

3. Christian Wolff, "Under the Influence," *TriQuarterly*, no. 54 (Spring 1982): 147.

4. John Cage, *Indeterminacy: New Aspects of Form in Instrumental and Electronic Music* (New York: Folkways, 1959), sound recording FT 3704.

Cage and the Antilogic of the Text ❑

What seems most important in this relatively matter-of-fact autobiographical anecdote, and in Cage's work as a whole, is not so much the communication of crucial narrative information as the demonstration of a crucial, unpredictable mode of narrative *process*. In a sense, Cage's aesthetic hinges upon a reversal of Barthes's early claim that narrative conveys little more than the structural logic of the text.[1] What appears to count for Cage is precisely the *antilogic* of the text, or that complex process by

41

which verbal narratives, ordered both according to grammar and according to variable speeds within units of fixed duration, coalesce with randomly ordered musical materials and evince the "coexistence of dissimilars" that Cage's address on "Experimental Music" (1958) associates with "a harmony to which many are unaccustomed" (*Silence*, 12).

Cage's concern with the temporal (or musical) organization of language (and sound) emerges in his 1948 lecture, "Defence of Satie," in which he postulates that duration is the most fundamental of musical qualities, reasoning,

> If you consider that sound is characterized by its pitch, its loudness, its timbre, and its duration, and that silence, which is the opposite and, therefore, the necessary partner of sound, is characterized only by its duration, you will be drawn to the conclusion that of the four characteristics of the material of music, duration, that is time length, is the most fundamental.[2]

As Cage subsequently explains in his notes to the recording of *Indeterminacy*, his performance of some seventy stories depends upon the rule of taking one minute to read each story, regardless of its length. In this respect, his slightly impersonal register fluctuates in terms of both its own accent or grain and in terms of the collectively established meter that Lyotard associates with primitive storytelling and that Jameson likewise seems to associate with third world literature, gossip, and "things of this kind."

There is no denying Cage's interest in, and assimilation of, Oriental narrative patterns, such as the haiku poetry that he admires for its "plurality of intention."[3] Cage's notes to *Indeterminacy* freely admit that some of the stories read during this work come from Kwang-Tse and Sri Ramakrishna and "the literature surrounding Zen."[4] Nevertheless, Cage is not simply a neo-primitive, appropriating third world materials in a pseudo–third world rhetoric. On the contrary, Cage intermingles a wide range of third world and first world materials both by orchestrating them according to the variously systematic and variously unsystematic schemata peculiar to Cageian composition and by modifying, superimposing, fragmenting, and conflating these materials by means of contemporary recording technology.

Both of these aspects of Cage's aesthetic—its play with duration and its use of studio technology—conveniently find exemplification in Cage's account of the initial difficulties in recording *Indeterminacy*. When his recording engineer complained, "You shouldn't pause the way you do between words; you should speak naturally," Cage reiterated his rationale for the "decentred" narrative in this work, explaining, "But this is what I have to do. I tell one story a minute, and, when it's a short one, I have to spread it out. Later on, when I come to a long one, I have to speak as rapidly as I can."[5]

Cage's more recent experiments are even more extreme in their endeavor to effect the "transition from language to music," and as Cage observes, they explore "nonsyntactical writing," which Cage would render as "empty of intention" and of precise meaning as musical sounds.[6] *Indeterminacy*, however, merely orchestrates words within micro-units of one minute's duration and within the macro-units of silence and live or electronic accompaniment that variously facilitate, complement, obscure, or obliterate Cage's variously paced utterances. Remarking upon the way in which a woman in the audience asked, "What, then is your final goal?" Cage's notes insist upon his indifference to the individual mind and emphasize his aspiration to enter a more collective, "eternal process":

> I observed that her question was that of the John Simon Guggenheim Memorial Foundation to applicants for fellowships, and that it had irritated artists for decades. Then I said that I did not see that we were going to a goal, but that we were living in process, and that process is eternal. My intention in putting 90 stories together in an unplanned way is to suggest that all things, sounds, stories (and, by extension, beings), *are* related, and that this complexity is more evident when it is not over-simplified by an idea of relationship in one person's mind.[7]

The quality of Cage's aesthetic becomes particularly clear if it is contrasted with that of Beckett. Whereas Beckett regrets that "the kind of work I do is one in which I'm not master of my material,"[8] Cage's writings repeatedly insist that so far as it is possible, Cage does not wish to be master of his material, given

43

the limitations that he perceives within "an idea of relationship in one person's mind." Accordingly, Cage emphasizes, for example, that "I try to arrange my composing means so that I won't have any knowledge of what might happen," adding, "I like to think . . . that I'm outside the circle of a known universe and dealing with things I literally don't know anything about."[9]

Notes

1. Roland Barthes, "Introduction to the Structural Analysis of Narratives" (1966), in *Image-Music-Text*, 124.
2. John Cage, "Defence of Satie" (1948), in *John Cage*, 81.
3. John Cage, "Conversation with Richard Kostelanetz" (1979), in *The Old Poetries and the New*, by Richard Kostelanetz (Ann Arbor: Univ. of Michigan Press, 1981), 255.
4. Cage, unpaginated notes for *Indeterminacy*.
5. Cage, *Indeterminacy* notes.
6. Cage, "Conversation with Kostelanetz," in *Old Poetries* 254, 267, 254.
7. Cage, *Indeterminacy* notes.
8. Beckett, qtd. in "Moody Man of Letters," by Shenker, 3.
9. John Cage, qtd. in " 'Live' Electronic Music," by Richard Teitelbaum, in *John Cage*, 141.

Beckett, Cage, and Nothing ❑

Not surprisingly, Cage's enthusiasm for unplanned, unknown modes of composition renders him indifferent to the Beckettian complaint that "there are many ways in which the thing I am trying in vain to say may be tried in vain to be said."[1] Whilst Beckett regrets that he can say nothing effectively, despite his "obligation to express," because "there is nothing to express, nothing with which to express, nothing from which to express,"[2] Cage neutralizes this problem with the jubilant assertion, *"I have nothing to say, and I am saying it and that is poetry as I need it"* (*Silence*,109; emphasis added).

Far from deploring that there are "no vehicles of communication" for what Beckett terms "valid expressions of the personality," Cage's conviction that "personality is a flimsy thing on which to build an art" (*Silence*, 90) leads to his celebration of *nothing* as the freedom that liberates the perceiver from the personality and all of its limiting *somethings*.[3] Thus, whereas Beckettian characters, such as Watt, can only suffer before the ambiguity and imprecision of what appears to be "a thing that was nothing," which they may neither explain nor "saddle . . . with meaning," Cage argues that poetry only begins when one abandons the attempt to possess reality by saddling it with meaning.[4] Cage's "Lecture on Nothing" (1959) concludes, "Our poetry now is the realization that we possess nothing. Anything therefore is a delight (since we do not possess it) and thus need not fear its loss" (*Silence*, 110).

Notes

1. Beckett, *Proust and Three Dialogues*, 123.
2. Beckett, *Proust and Three Dialogues*, 103.
3. Beckett, *Proust and Three Dialogues*, 64.
4. Beckett, *Watt*, 76, 73, 75.

Beckett, Cage, and Programmatic Composition ❏

The difference between Beckett's and Cage's variants of postmodern aesthetics and creativity is obviously a question of degree rather than any absolute dichotomy. As I have suggested, Cage's work, like Beckett's work, generates its own highly individual punctum. Similarly, Beckett's fiction frequently explores modes of impersonal composition. Nevertheless, as becomes evident when one contrasts the "sucking-stone" incident in Beckett's *Molloy* (1959) and Cage's notes on *Construction in Metal* (1939), the existential and aesthetic implications of Beckett's and Cage's use of programmatic composition differ considerably. Initially, Molloy's anticipation of his "chances of enjoying" the distribution of sixteen stones through his four pockets, "turn and turn about, as I wished," has much in common with Cage's systematic concerns in *Construction in Metal*.[1] Noting that his choice of sounds in this work "had in mind that they should be sixteen for each player," Cage explains,

> The number sixteen was also that of the number of measures of four-four in each unit of the rhythmic structure. . . . The plan, as preconceived, was to use four of the sounds in the first sixteen measures, introducing in each succeeding structural unit four more until the exposition involving all sixteen and lasting through the first four units was completed. (*Silence*, 23)

Beckett's Molloy, of course, employs his permutations of sixteen units through four spaces as a means of *control* and of determining—"as I wished" (70)—"the distribution of the sixteen stones in groups of four, one group in each pocket" (71). As Molloy admits, the "heartbreaking stages" of his permutations not only lack a certain elegance, insofar as "the only perfect solution" would have been "sixteen pockets, symmetrically disposed, each one with its stone" (73) but also appear quite inconsequential, since he "didn't give a fiddler's curse" and finally chose "to throw away all the stones but one" (74).

Cage concedes that the first performance of *Construction in Metal* suffered from a similar inelegance, insofar as "one of the players used three Japanese temple gongs rather than four" (*Silence*, 24), while "the addition of metal thundersheets" brought "the number sixteen, for those players who enjoyed it to seventeen" (24–25). Significantly, though, Cage's response to these deviations from his plan is indulgent rather than impatient. Cage cheerfully justifies the use of three Japanese temple gongs (rather than the projected four) on the grounds that "the fact that only three of these relatively rare instruments were available to me, together with the attachment I felt toward their sound . . . convinced me of the rightness of this change in number" (24). Cage offered similar tolerance toward those players whose attachment to metal thundersheets led them to increase their number from sixteen to seventeen.

While he admits that these inconsistencies might suggest that *Construction in Metal* was "imperfectly realized" (25), such notional imperfections seem secondary to Cage's enthusiasm for the ways in which this performance revealed "interesting differences between certain of these sounds" (25). Accordingly, Cage defends imperfectly realized art as an aspect of "purposeful purposelessness" and "purposeful play" rather than abandoning his compositions without even a fiddler's curse, like Beckett's Molloy, and rather than deeming such compositional inelegance yet another example of the "coming and going in purposelessness" deplored by the Beckettian protagonist.[2] Meditating upon the purpose of art and music, Cage's address on "Experimental Music" (1958) contends,

> One is, of course, not dealing with purposes but dealing with sounds. Or the answer must take the form of a paradox: a purposeful purposelessness or a purposeless play. This play, however, is an affirmation of life—not an attempt to bring order out of chaos or to suggest improvements in creation, but simply a way of waking up to the very life we're living, which is so excellent once one gets one's mind and one's desires out of the way and lets it act of its own accord. (*Silence*, 12)

Notes

1. Samuel Beckett, *Molloy*, in *Molloy, Malone Dies, The Unnamable* (1959; rpt., London: John Calder, 1966), 70. All subsequent references to *Molloy* appear in the text.
2. Beckett, *Watt*, 57.

Purposeful Purposelessness or Nothing to Be Done? ❑

Cage's suggestion that one should let life "act of its own accord" and moreover, that "the very life we're living" can be "so excellent" hints that an unexpected silver lining may lie behind the cloudy Beckettian dictum, "Nothing to be done."[1]

Negating the nihilism of the B-effect, the C-effect of Cage's postmodern aesthetic transforms this negative imperative into the surprisingly positive process of getting "one's mind and one's desires out of the way."

Cage attributes two main advantages to this positive transcendence of the mind and of desires. Firstly, he reasons that since "the highest purpose is to have no purpose," such positive purposelessness places one "in accord with nature in her manner of operation" (*Silence*, 155). Secondly, he postulates that positively purposeless creativity also puts art in accord with nature by precipitating organic coherence. This point becomes particularly explicit in Cage's "Defence of Satie," (1948), a lecture in which Cage defines both the function of music and his own general aesthetic, in terms of his wish

> to bring into co-being elements paradoxical by nature, to bring into one situation elements that can be and ought to be agreed upon—that is, law elements—together with elements that cannot and ought not to be agreed upon—that is, freedom elements—these two ornamented by other elements, which may lend support to one or the other of the two fundamental and opposed elements, *the whole forming thereby an organic unity* (emphasis added).[2]

Some forty years after their first pronouncement at Black Mountain College, Cage's words remain astonishingly pertinent to any understanding of the positive dimension of the postmodern aesthetic. First and foremost, Cage intimates that art need not "fail, as no other dare fail" but may precipitate unanticipated forms of organic unity by juxtaposing paradoxical elements within compositions that may initially appear nothing more than *anti*-art, resisting past conventions, but which, upon more patient inspection, prove to be the constituents of *ante*-art, generating new conventions. Secondly, as Cage's variously technological experiments demonstrate, his aesthetic emerges from the heart of the age of hypermechanical reproduction and production, at the very forefront of the peculiarly positive American creativity that this book associates with postmodernism's C-effect.

Notes

1. Beckett, *Waiting for Godot*, 9.
2. John Cage, "Defence of Satie," 84.

Jameson, Bourdieu, and the Destruction of Art and Taste ❑

Despite his present objections to exclusively technological compositions existing in permanent *reel* time as recordings—rather than as live performances in *real* time—on the grounds that "music is actually a process that's never twice the same" and that "record listeners are not really prepared for listening to live music," Cage's general enthusiasm for the postmodern media refreshingly repudiates the sporadically Luddite quality of Benjamin's, Barthes's, Bonita-Oliva's, and Bürger's responses to contemporary technology.[1] One might well add Pierre Bourdieu's name to this list, insofar as Jameson's readings of *Un art mineur* persuade him that "Bourdieu demystifies all theories of aesthetic value" and "unmasks *all* . . . theories of cultural value" as "so much Sartrean bad faith in the services of class activities and class praxis of a nonaesthetic nature," thereby effecting "the destruction of categories of 'taste' and 'art.' "[2]

Jameson's notional addition to the diverse "obituaries" announced in, and culled from, "B" writings derives from Bourdieu's hypothesis that whereas " 'realistic' photography belongs primarily to the practices of . . . the family," where it is used for the portraits that Bourdieu associates with "the social reproduction of the family," those who employ photography "for specifically 'artistic' reasons are, in sociological terms, marginals: bachelors, young people, unsuccessful 'family men' " escaping the family and affirming a different kind of identity.[3]

Bourdieu subdivides such marginals into two categories: firstly, those who assume the "technological apologia" of being "interested in the machinery and its possibilities" and secondly,

49

those who assume the " 'aesthetic' (or perhaps we should say the 'symbolist') apologia." This second grouping allegedly associate photography with "various idiosyncratic experiences of beauty" and explain their activities by analogy with "the established languages and rationales of the older (aristocratic) high art" in theories "contaminated with the traditions of high culture" and "socially and institutionally grounded in the bourgeois social order itself."[4]

Notes

1. The quotes are from John Cage, interview with Tom Darter, *Keyboard*, 8.9 (Sept. 1982): 21.
2. Jameson, "Hans Haacke," 44, 45. Jameson paraphrases Pierre Bourdieu's *Un art mineur* (Paris: Minuit 1965).
3. Jameson, "Hans Haacke," 44.
4. Jameson, "Hans Haacke," 45.

Chion, Cage, and New Aesthetic Rationales ❑

Jameson's summary of Bourdieu's "devastating" theories has a certain tautological inevitability. All aesthetical arguments are, it seems, contaminated by class interest because they all invariably conform to the "socially and institutionally grounded" rationales of the "older (aristocratic) high arts."

By contrast, Michel Chion's analyses of the adjacent fields of cinema and electroacoustic music suggest that Bourdieu's analyses overlook, or underlook, the ways in which new art forms, such as photography, not only lend themselves to definition in terms of earlier aesthetic rationales and naive modes of technological apologia but also explore profoundly new aesthetic rationales. According to Chion, new media initially provoke the elementary technological experiments that he associates with "zero" experiments (and which seem to exemplify the naive technological apologia) and then subsequently precipitate "imitative" works that employ new media according to previous conventions (such as the aristocratic aesthetic discussed by Bourdieu).[1]

Chion departs most radically from Bourdieu's schemata when he identifies his third mode of artistic experimentation: "purist" experimentation, or the exploration of the new media in terms of their own particular logic.[2] This is precisely the kind of activity that Cage advocates in his article entitled "Experimental Music: Doctrine" (1955), when he argues that experimentation with recording tape can completely transform one's aesthetic assumptions, so long as one does not attempt to employ or justify such experimentation in terms of previous conventions. Cage observes,

> Magnetic tape opens the door providing one doesn't immediately shut it by . . . [using] it to recall or extend known musical possibilities. It introduces the unknown with such sharp clarity that anyone has the opportunity of having his habits blown away like dust. (*Silence*, 16)

Four years later, Cage's article "History of Experimental Music in the United States" similarly advocated the exploration of the electronic media pioneered by Varèse, avowing, "One is no longer concerned with tonality or atonality . . . nor with consonance and dissonance, but rather with Edgard Varèse who fathered forth noise into twentieth century music" (*Silence*, 69). Specifying that the new electronic noises and tones identified by Varèse should now be considered impersonally, in their own right, with "a kind of objectivity, almost anonymity" (68), Cage concludes, "It is clear that ways must be discovered that allow noises and tones to be just noises and tones, not exponents subservient to Varèse's imagination" (69).

Notes

1. Michel Chion, "Vingt années de musique électroacoustique ou une quête d'identité," *Musique en jeu*, no. 8 (Sept. 1972): 26–27.
2. Chion, "Vingt années," 27.

Over and over again, this "purist" impulse informs postmodern theory and postmodern creativity. At its most basic, it prompts the endeavor to reassess familiar materials in their own right, irrespective of their referential implications. Barthes, for example, argues that "narrative . . . is simply there, like life itself" and proposes that "in the multiplicity of writing, everything is to be *disentangled,* nothing *deciphered.*"[1] Composed some half-dozen years before Barthes's meditations upon the structural properties of narrative and upon the death of the author, the American composer La Monte Young's "Lecture 1960" similarly observed, "If we try to enslave some of the sounds and force them to obey our will, they become useless. . . . If, however, we go to the sounds as they exist and try to experience them for what they are . . . then we may be able to learn something new."[2]

Still more significant, however, are those artists who attempt to explore the unknown aesthetic potential of the emergent postmodern media. Kinetic artists such as the American Frank Malina have worked with luminous compositions born of the incandescent bulb, the fluorescent tube, and "silent electronic motors of small dimension," an art for which, as Malina observes, "aesthetic guide lines . . . have not yet been formulated."[3] Audio poets, such as the French writer/composer Henri Chopin, have in turn explored "sound poetry, made for and by the tape-recorder," and therefore "more easily codified by machines and electricity . . . than any means proper to writing."[4]

More recently, telecommunications artists such as the Englishman Roy Ascott have explored *telematics,* or the interactive, collaborative art born of "telecommunications and computers," which Ascott hails as "a paradigm change in our culture" and as "a quantum leap in human consciousness," revealing "new possibilities of mind and new intimations of reality" by breaking "the boundaries not only of the insular individual but of institutions, territories and time zones."[5] Considered in the terminology of Félix Guattari, the purist experiments of Cage, Malina, Chopin, Ascott, and other astronauts of electronic space demystify the mythologies of the B-effect—and more particularly, the mythologies that Guattari associates with "the structuralist straightjacket"—and "make it possible to accede to changing creative realms" through "the miniaturization and personalization of machinery" and the "re-singularization of mechanically mediated means of expression."[6]

As Michel Chion observes, purist innovations exploring new modes of purist aesthetic peculiar to this or that exploration of "mechanically mediated expression" are frequently followed by a final mode of synthesis, incorporating both past and present discourses within "hybrid" compositions.[7] It might be tempting to conceive of such works as being "contaminated" by the prior codes and conventions of traditional "class interest" (to reiterate the terms of Jameson's paean to Bourdieu). But as Chion suggests, such hybrid works self-consciously interweave past and present aesthetics from the point of view of the most recent present, with all the advantages of hindsight afforded by purist experimentation. In this respect, hybrid works are not so much instances of contamination or chaos but rather the considered integration of the old and the new within "changing creative realms."

Notes

1. Barthes, "Introduction to the Structural Analysis of Narratives," 79; "Death of the Author," 147.
2. La Monte Young, "Excerpts from 'Lecture 1960,' " *Kulchur* 3.10 (Summer 1963): 18–19.
3. Frank J. Malina, "Kinetic Painting: The Lumidyne System" (1968), in *Kinetic Art: Theory and Practice*, ed. Malina (New York: Dover, 1974), 37, 45.
4. Henri Chopin, "Open Letter to Aphonic Musicians" (1967), trans. Jean Ratcliffe-Chopin, *OU*, no. 33 (1968): 11. All subsequent references to "Open Letter" appear in the text.
5. Roy Ascott, "Art and Telematics," in *Art + Telecommunication*, ed. Heidi Grundmann (Vienna: BLIX, 1984), 33, 57.
6. Félix Guattari, "The Postmodern Dead End," trans.

Nancy Blake, *Flash Art* (international ed.), no. 128 (May/June 1986): 41.

    7. Chion, "Vingt années," 27.

Postmodernism's Hybrid Aesthetic ❑

American postmodern creativity of the last quarter century appears to exemplify precisely this kind of considered "hybrid" creativity. In Cage's case, his work-in-progress, *Europera*, involves a complex amalgam of theatrical, musical, and operatic materials coexisting and interchanging within a slightly more restrained variant of the interactive cybernetic space that Roy Ascott associates with telecommunications. Cage explains,

> I'm also working on *Europera*, an opera without a libretto. There's no plot. It's a collage of all the theatrical elements, and nothing is related intentionally to anything else. . . . I think that what happens, both in succession and simultaneously can be said to be surprising and unexpected. It's actually in a form of theater with which I'm unfamiliar. I look forward to experiencing it.[1]

Crucial here seem to be Cage's enthusiasm for the surprising, the unexpected and unfamiliar, and his implicit conviction that the notionally anarchic materials of *Europera* will in fact intermingle, however unpredictably, into some sort of new theater. Here, then, one encounters the essence of hybrid American postmodernity and the essence of what we have termed the C-effect: a confident commitment to the positive, organic synthesis of antilinear or multilinear modes of traditional creativity and multimedia creativity.

As the following discussion will suggest, the emergence of the C-effect aesthetic is often far more ambiguous in Europe than in America, whereas two generations of innovative multimedia artists such as Cage, Ashley and Gaburo, and Glass, Wilson, and Anderson confirm Cage's assertion that the most positive postmodern souls are "conveniently electric."[2] While the work of technological European artists such as the sound poet Henri Chopin and the kinetic artists documented by Frank Popper's monumental *Electra* exhibition of 1983 indicate that American multimedia creativity has obvious European counterparts, the work of other writers, theorists, and artists such as Beuys, Eco, Grass, Wolf, and Müller suggests the ways in which postmodern European creativity often culminates in more retrospective, primitive, or shamanistic variants of the C-effect.

Notes

1. Cage, *Eyeline*, 6.
2. Cage, *John Cage*, 167.

Feldman, Crazy Contradiction, and the Conceptual, Artistic Life ❏

According to Cage's friend and fellow composer Morton Feldman, European and American creativity in the sixties displays two general traits, the first of these being an American rejection of overly mechanical theory in favor of the retention of some sort of performative presence. Feldman explains:

> There is still an incredible difference between Europe and America. In Europe what is presented is really a machine, and the human being who is doing it is left out of it—he's out of it because he's surrendered to a conceptual, artistic life. Now, in New York, with myself, and much of the painting of the fifties, the man himself . . . gives you this art without this dialectical justification. What it really amounts to is whether you want to be in the work, in the medium, or outside it. . . . I feel that Cage and myself are in the work.[1]

This rejection of explicit dialectical justification and of overly conceptual creativity seems accompanied by an American acceptance of everyday modes of surrealistic contradiction within the environment. In other words, no hard and fast contrast is necessarily conceptualized between the real and the surreal, the mundane and the marvelous. Rather than dwelling upon the conceptual incompatibility of seemingly contradictory perceptions, the American C-effect apparently interweaves and accepts the copresence of differing discourses and conflicting categories: art and life, high culture and low culture, order and disorder, anonymity and subjectivity.

Thus, somewhat as Warhol celebrates the comedy of everyday catastrophes in the Bowery, Feldman confides that his antipathy to the environment of New York—and his sense that it was just "a big bore"—gradually gave way to discovery of its "almost crazy contradiction." Discussing his conversion to the ecstasy of the moment (as opposed to a sense of vulnerability to the tyranny of the moment), Feldman continues,

> I remember I was having a lesson with Wolpe and he had a studio on 14th Street. It's the proleterian's 5th Avenue and so Wolpe liked it. He was very socially orientated and he was talking about the man in the street and I was getting a scolding, and I was looking out of the window and there I saw crossing the street Jackson Pollock. I didn't say a word to Wolpe and he went on talking about the man in the street. But there was that crazy almost surrealistic contradiction. It was almost as if Jackson just came by just to get me out of this particular dilemma.[2]

Notes

1. Morton Feldman, interview with Alan Beckett, *International Times* (London), no. 3 (1966): 7.
2. Feldman, *International Times*, 7.

Pure "H"—Habermas and
Communicative Rationality ☐

Morton Feldman's reference to the predominantly conceptual quality of European artistic life and his suggestion that the American sensibility inhabits a more open realm of surrealistic contradiction economically exemplify one of the key tensions within both European and American theoretical and creative practices: the antithesis between predominantly rational and predominantly extrarational points of departure, or in Burroughs's terms, the dichotomy between conscious control and less predictable modes of "letting things happen in their own way without interference" (*Dead Fingers Talk*, 20).

Rather than exhibiting any crude nationalistic or geographic patterns of difference, European and American variants of the postmodern sensibility seem to diverge most obviously in terms of the variable emphasis that their initial conceptual parameters and expectations place upon rational and extrarational knowledge frames. Among those European writings advertently or inadvertently contributing to the reductive rationalism that these pages associate with the postmodern sensibility's B-effect, Jurgen Habermas's account of the relationship between "aesthetic modernity" and "the project of modernity formulated in the 18th century by the philosophers of the Enlightenment" offers one of the most striking examples of what Feldman calls the European conceptual mentality.[1] Redefining the European modernist project not so much in terms of what he dismisses as "the usual concentration upon art" as in terms of the more general social and cultural aspirations of the Enlightenment philosophers, Habermas defines *modernity* as the attempt to "develop objective science, universal morality and law, and autonomous art according to their inner logic" ("Modernity," 8). As Habermas stipulates, this project aspires to release the cognitive potentials of each of these domains from their esoteric forms . . . [and] . . . to utilize this accumulation of specialized culture for the enrichment of everyday life—that is to say, for the rational organization of everyday social life" (9).

57

This argument leads Habermas to what one might term his "pure-'H' imperative": unconditional "adherence to what I call communicative rationality" ("Modernity," 8). This imperative in turn seems to provoke unconditional rejection of any mode of communicative *irrationality* or *extrarationality*, particularly those aspects of "aesthetic modernity" (5) that Habermas finds "altogether incompatible with the moral basis of a purposive, rational conduct of life" (6).

High on Habermas's hit list of incompatible modes of modernist art are "the hopeless surrealist revolts" ("Modernity," 13). According to pure Habermasian communicative rationality, the hopelessness of these revolts was doubly inevitable. First, surrealist works fatally disrupt rational discourse. Accordingly, "an emancipatory effect does not follow." Rationally speaking, "nothing remains from a desublimated meaning or destructured form" (11). Secondly, surrealist art is literally just that—surrealist art—rather than "a cultural tradition covering all spheres—cognitive, moral-practical and expressive." In this respect, it only influences "a single cultural sphere—art" and utterly fails to fulfill the Enlightenment project's mission to save "rationalized everyday life" as a whole from "cultural impoverishment" (11).

To be sure, surrealist polemic does at times claim to afford "the solution of the principal problems of life" (as Breton asserts, for example, in his "Surrealist Manifesto" (1924).[2] Nevertheless, to carp at the literal contradictions in such avant-garde manifestos is to miss the point that they quite self-consciously intermingle serious intent with provocative overstatement. *Literally* speaking, as Habermas rather tiresomely reminds us, "all those attempts to level art and life . . . [and] . . . to declare everything to be art and everyone to be an artist . . . have proved themselves to be sort of nonsense experiments" ("Modernity," 10). Breton's aspirations certainly taunt the reader with extravagant claims. But as Breton subsequently indicates in "What Is Surrealism?" (1934), his actual expectations were frequently far more modest than their rhetorical flourishes. Looking forward to "the future transmutation of these two seemingly contradictory states, dream and reality, into a sort of absolute reality," Breton adds, "I am looking forward to its consummation, certain that I shall never share in it."[3]

Arguably, Habermas confuses Breton's bark with his bite. One might similarly respond, somewhat overliterally, that Habermas's own wish to level art and life by declaring everything and everyone amenable to amelioration by "the rational organization of everyday social life" constitutes an equally improbable nonsense experiment. Given the way of the world, the aspiration to infuse communicative rationality across *all* spheres of society seems extremely optimistic.

In this respect, Habermas seems to oppose Breton's surrealist shamanism with the Enlightenment tradition's rationalist shamanism. While one can share Habermas's enthusiasm for "purposive, rational conduct" ("Modernity," 6), excessive commitment to this ideal distracts one from the alternative advantages of what Cage's "Experimental Music" paradoxically terms "purposeful purposelessness" (*Silence*, 12). To reiterate Cage's argument, such purposeless play evades the temptation "to bring order out of chaos or to suggest improvements in creation" and advocates instead a more general acceptance of "the very life we're living, which is so excellent once one gets one's mind and one's desires out of the way and lets it act of its own accord" (12).

As Donald Kuspit indicates in "Beuys, Fat, Felt, and Alchemy" (in *The Critic Is Artist*), Habermas's compatriot, the artist Joseph Beuys, makes much the same point when he proposes a third form of discourse, beyond both "atavistic shamanism" and "atavistic science," that consolidates shamanistic confidence in "a possibility for historical development" by exploring "another stage of development in our relationship to material."[4]

For all its positive intentions, Habermas's assessment of modernist and postmodernist culture pivots—(like Bürger's *Theory of the Avant-Garde*, a book to which Habermas approvingly alludes)—upon the B-effect myth that "we are experiencing the end of the idea of modern art" and that in the wake of "the failure of the surrealist rebellion," the avant-garde is "supposedly no longer creative" ("Modernity," 6).

Notes

1. Jurgen Habermas, "Modernity versus Post-Modernity," *New German Critique*, no. 22 (Winter 1981): 5, 9. All subsequent references to this essay appear in the text.

2. André Breton, discusses his "Surrealist Manifesto" (1924), in his essay "What Is Surrealism?" (1934), trans. David Gascoyne, in *Theories of Modern Art*, 412.

3. Breton, "What Is Surrealism?" 414.

4. Joseph Beuys, qtd. in *The Critic Is Artist: The Intentionality of Art*, by Donald Kuspit (Ann Arbor, Mich.: U.M.I. Research Press, 1984), 352. All subsequent references to this work appear in the text.

Beuys, Adorno, and the Silence of Marcel Duchamp ❑

Like Habermas, Beuys argues that "the period of modern art ended in Germany with the beginning of the Hitler era."[1] Unlike Habermas, Beuys advocates a fusion of rational and extra-rational knowledges and creativity. As Beuys specifies in his address "Talking about One's Own Country: Germany" (1985), he envisages art both as "a newborn child of the old disciplines" and as "social art, social sculpture, which sets itself the task of apprehending more than just physical material" by emerging from "spiritual soil."[2]

Beuys certainly shares Habermas's conviction that art should cover "all spheres—cognitive, moral-practical and expressive." But to these Habermasian categories he adds both the spiritual sphere and the democratic imperative that "everyone is an artist" in the sense that "every single person both can and even must participate" in the "re-shaping of the social body" ("Talking," 39). Outlining his views in an interview with Willoughby Sharp of 1969, Beuys explains:

> I demand an artistic involvement in all realms of life. At the moment, art is taught as a special field which demands the production of documents in the form of art works. Whereas I

advocate an aesthetic involvement from science, from economics, from politics, from religion—every sphere of human activity. Even the act of peeling a potato can be a work of art if it is a conscious act.[3]

What Beuys seems to imply here is not so much that a peeled potato is an artwork, but that life may be positively leveled when all actions are undertaken with the higher responsibility that he defines as *aesthetic involvement*. With this maxim in mind, Beuys repeatedly argued that the key task for humanity is to undertake every activity *artistically*. Tracing his own development from the scientific determinism that one might associate with the B-effect to the more metaphysical values of what I would term the C-effect, Beuys suggested to Willoughby Sharp that "the crux of the matter is that my work is permeated with thoughts that do not originate in the official development of art but in scientific concepts":

> You know, to begin with I wanted to be a scientist. But I found that the theoretical structure of the natural sciences was too positivist for me, so I tried to do something new for both science and art. I wanted to widen both areas. . . . in the simplest terms I am trying to reaffirm the concept of art and creativity in the face of Marxist doctrine. The Socialist movements in Europe which are now strongly supported by the young constantly provoke this question. They define man exclusively as a social being. I wasn't surprised by this development, which led to the confused political conditions not only in Germany but also in America. Man really is not free in many respects. He is dependent on his social circumstances, but he is free in his thinking. . . . My theory depends on the fact that every human being is an artist. I have to encounter him when he is free, when he is thinking. ("Interview with Sharp," 90–91)

Continuing in self-consciously abstract terms, Beuys explained to Sharp that this process of heightened thinking replicates the same sort of transition "from the chaotic principle to the form principle" that his *Fettecke* (corners of fat) sculptures represent, as "fat in liquid form distributes itself chaotically in an undifferentiated fashion until it collects in a different form in a corner" ("Interview with Sharp," 91). Beuys acknowledges

that such symbolic transition cannot be understood in materialistic terms. Rather, it requires the spectator to be moved subcon-
sciously, a condition which makes the more materialistic viewer
"react angrily and destroy my work and curse it" (85–86).

This is certainly the case. If Beuys's suggestions that the
process of peeling the potato "can be a work of art" is guaranteed
to activate the Habermasian charge of "nonsense," his use of
unsightly wedges of fat to symbolize what Donald Kuspit terms
"the redemptive power of chaos" (*Critic Is Artist*, 151) proves
even more irritating to many of his critics. As Kuspit points
out, Beuys seems to suggest that his corners of fat incarnate a
positive metamorphosis from chaos into form, counterbalancing
and perhaps compensating for the more historically specific
negative conversion of "human flesh (order) into soap fat
(chaos)" at Auschwitz. Despite his sympathy for Beuys's metaphoric vision, Kuspit asks the rather more literal question:
"How can Beuys's fat redeem Auschwitz's fat?"(351), and he
concludes that Beuys's alchemical imagery probably works best
in a specifically German context, insofar as it

> takes a risk that perhaps only Germans—or at least not Ameri-
> cans, who have not had such a socially devastating experi-
> ence—can understand. He attempts to come to terms with his
> country's—and his own—historical experience, so as not to
> repeat it. . . . Beuys metaphorically repeats the past in order
> to avoid its literal repetition in some future, however remote.
> (357)

Whether Beuys's metaphorical imagery is effective or not, it
seems evident that he breaks with two of the most enduring
negative taboos of late modernism, and two of the key mythologies contributing to the B-effect. Firstly, he challenges Adorno's
assumption—or directive—that there can be "no poetry after
Auschwitz," and as Kuspit puts it, he attempts "to come to
terms with a range of experience—the holocaust—which is still
a nearly taboo subject to many people who think that there is
no way of rationalizing it, even with the aid of the magic of art"
(*Critic Is Artist*, 357).

As Beuys relates to William Furlong, he also rejects the

concomitant "cancer" of negative and nihilistic theories of post-modern art, along with the whole notion of "modern" art, in favor of the redemptive "anthropological art" that he associates with "humankind's creative structures and senses" and with "thought, feeling and the giving of power."[4] To quote from another of Beuys's interviews, this time with Richard Demarco in 1982, his art combines both a general sense of "spiritual necessity" and a "reasonable, practical anthropology" responding to specific existing systems.[5]

To take but one example, Beuys's decision to incarcerate himself with a coyote in his performance *Coyote: I Like America and America Likes me* (1974) typifies his sensitivity both to the anthropological symbolic impact of the "invisible powers" associated with animals and the more immediate culturally specific impact of the coyote—a creature, as Caroline Tisdall remarks, "respected and venerated by the Red Man, despised and persecuted by the White Man" and as such, the perfect emblem for what Beuys termed "the whole American Trauma with the Indian, the Red Man."[6]

Far from confirming the B-effect mythology of the impossibility of commenting upon the postwar social order in Germany—or indeed, elsewhere—Beuys consistently directed public attention toward his polemical, sculptural, or gestural responses to sensitive social issues. Not simply what Kuspit calls "a barker for spiritualism" (*Critic Is Artist*, 356), Beuys was also very much a barker barking against quite specific examples of "bad positions in the social order."

At the same time, Beuys also made it his business to challenge the second great negative myth of modernist art history: *The Silence of Marcel Duchamp.* Rather than accepting that there could be "no art after Duchamp's urinal," Beuys declared that "the silence of Marcel Duchamp is over-rated," remarking to Furlong that whereas Duchamp had "tried to destroy the rule of tradition towards something else with his pissoir piece" and was "really interested in the transformation of art," he "did not transform it" because he finally "wanted to become a hero in silence or in saying nothing or resigning his whole idea of art." Distinguishing his own redemptive anti-art from Duchamp's unredemptive silence, Beuys adds: "I try to go further on over the threshold where modern art ends and anthropological art has to start."[7]

Notes

1. Joseph Beuys, "Plight," interview with William Furlong, *Art Monthly*, no. 112 (Dec. 1987/Jan. 1988): 7.
2. Joseph Beuys, "Talking about One's Own Country: Germany" (1985), trans. Timothy Nevil, in *In Memoriam Joseph Beuys: Obituaries, Essays, Speeches* (Bonn: Inter Nationes, 1986), 38. All subsequent references to this essay appear in the text.
3. Joseph Beuys, "Interview with Willoughby Sharp" (1969), in *Energy Plan for Western Man/Joseph Beuys in America: Writings by and with the Artist*, ed. Carin Kuoni (New York: Four Walls Eight Windows, 1990), 87. All subsequent references to this interview appear in the text. (Henceforth, the volume is abbreviated as *Joseph Beuys in America*.)
4. Beuys, "Plight," 7.
5. Joseph Beuys, "Interview with Richard Demarco" (1982), in *Joseph Beuys in America*, 115.
6. Caroline Tisdall, "Beuys: *Coyote*," *Studio International* 192.982 (July/Aug. 1976): 39.
7. Beuys, "Plight," 8.

Beuys, Cage, Buchloh, and the B-B Effect ❏

It is precisely the impulse to move beyond the blunt edge of prior discourse, where art "ends," to the cutting edge of innovative discourse where "art has to start," and—in Barthes's terms—where art is "born technically . . . even aesthetically" before being theorized and "born aesthetically,"[1] which characterizes Beuys's contribution to the postmodern C-effect. Whether this contribution should be theorized or defined as anthropological or as positively postmodern is of secondary significance. Like Cage's research, Beuys's art is most consequential as creative commitment to innovative possibilities "outside the circle of a known universe." Somewhat as Cage claims to be "dealing with things I literally don't know anything about,"[2] Beuys specifies that while he may "know a lot" before he starts an action, he neither knows nor desires to know "anything about the process in which the action will run" since

> it would be a very uninteresting thing—it would have nothing to do with art—if it were not a new experiment for which I have no clear concept. If I had a clear concept of solving the problem, I would then speak about the concept and it wouldn't be necessary to make an action. Every action, every art work for me, every physical scene, drawing on the blackboard, performance, brings a new element in the whole, an unknown area, an unknown world.[3]

When Willoughby Sharp asked, "Which artist do you feel close to?" Beuys tellingly responded, "John Cage," adding, "Perhaps the reason I love Cage and Nam June Paik . . . is because they are at the point of origin. Things have a certain reach. Beyond that everything is derivative" ("Interview with Sharp," 87). Beuys's insistence upon the possibility of such points of origin, despite the apparent demise of modern art in the Hitler period, epitomizes one of the key traits of the C-effect—the extralogical suspension of the logical disbelief that persuades B-effect thinkers like Habermas and Bürger that the avant-garde is no longer creative.

More significantly still, like many of the other American artists that this book will subsequently associate with the C-effect, Beuys proposes that his art looks beyond the limitations of surrealism. Contrary to the surrealists' assertion "that they could live with their subconscious . . . above reality," Beuys claims that they were frequently "beneath it." According to Beuys, many of surrealism's images have "a repressive effect," in the sense that their impact—like that of Duchamp's work— fails to provoke interest "in consciousness, in methodology, in serious historical discussion and analysis."[4]

Ironically, American-based carriers of the B-effect, such as the art historian Benjamin Buchloh—whose vehement intolerance towards the concept of the postmodern avant-garde culminates in what one might think of as the *B-B-effect*—reject Beuys's work for exactly the same reasons that Beuys himself criticizes surrealism and Duchamp. Beuys hoped that his critics would eventually say, "Beuys understood the historical situation. He altered the course of events" ("Interview with Sharp," 92). Buchloh, however, condemns Beuys's "program for the *Free International University*" as "simple-minded utopian drivel lacking elementary political and educational practicality" just as he dismisses Beuys's affirmation that everyone is an artist as "an obsolete surrealist statement" that "lacks any historical precision."[5] From Buchloh's point of view,

> Historical thought on any level—whether general historical thought, art-historical thought, any attempt to acknowledge the specific condition of a historical situation—is rejected by Beuys altogether. The history of post–Second-World-War Germany, which is Beuys's own historical situation; the history of an emerging, economically powerful society; the history of specific art forms—all of these are ignored, falsified, or mythified. ("Beuys at the Guggenheim," 11)

Focusing upon the notorious contradictions in Beuys's "mythified" autobiography, Buchloh condemns him above all for deploying the "fairly obsolete conception of the artist" operating "within an avant-garde condition" ("Beuys at the Guggenheim," 16). Refusing to contemplate counterparts to these strategies in the work of Cage and Duchamp, Buchloh abruptly—and rather amusingly—counters Annette Michelson's perceptive suggestion that Beuys "seems to play a role in Germany analogous to that of Cage" with the kneejerk response, "I would strongly oppose any alignment of Beuys with either Duchamp or Cage. I don't think that they can be compared at all. Neither Duchamp nor Cage consistently created that kind of myth" (12).

At a more general level, Buchloh condemns Beuys still more bitterly for offering the German spirit of the postwar period the means of "pardoning and reconciling itself prematurely with its own reminiscences of a responsibility for one of the most cruel and devastating forms of collective political madness that history has known."[6]

Buchloh's hostility toward Beuys thus derives from three subjective sources: his impatience before mythological discourse; his intolerance toward the concept of the unique, original artist; and his personal conviction that it is too soon to acknowledge the possibility of poetry—let alone redemptive poetry—after Auschwitz.

Put another way, Buchloh finds Beuys guilty of two conceptual heresies. First, Beuys "has never considered Habermas . . . nor any of the other social philosophers and historians who have grown out of the Frankfurt School . . . which would be an obvious thing to do if one were seriously concerned with political problems" ("Beuys at the Guggenheim," 43). Second, Beuys repeatedly expressed open "disapproval of Duchamp's Anti-art concept."[7] Still more culpably, Beuys apparently "dilutes and dissolves the conceptual precision of Duchamp's readymade by reintegrating the object into the most traditional and naive context of representation of meaning: the idealist metaphor," thereby condemning himself to a "state of obsolescence . . . within the discourse of art itself" ("Beuys at the Guggenheim," 39–40).

Like other B-effect theorists, Buchloh deplores the obsolescence of work that defies notions of historical precision drawn from the discourse of art itself ("Beuys at the Guggenheim," 40). In his turn, Beuys, like other C-effect artists, responds as best he may to "the necessity to change the understanding of science and art and to broaden the idea of points of reality." Rather than reiterating Habermasian rationality or the Duchampian discourse of art, Beuys attempts to define "my reality . . . another reality than the reality of the American modern art."[8]

Likewise, rather than sharing Buchloh's conviction that "you simply cannot perform the role of the saviour at the same time that you are operating within a highly calculated economic system" ("Beuys at the Guggenheim," 16), Beuys characteristically asserts, "Economic circumstances do not determine me. I determine them. Every man is a potential provocateur" ("Interview with Sharp," 86).

Collectively, Buchloh's B-B-effect blind spots prompt the conclusion that Beuys's provocations were merely the actions of "a fool or a very shrewd trickster . . . serving particular ends for the new German bourgeoisie" ("Beuys at the Guggenheim," 16). Arguably, the reverse obtains. By denying the validity of Beuys's work and by delegating it to the discourse of the fool or trickster, Buchloh discredits his challenges to the "new German bourgeoisie," reestablishes confidence in materialist values, and confirms the B-effect myth that utopian aspirations are somehow a thing of the past.

Notes

1. Barthes, "The Third Meaning," *Image-Music-Text*, 67.
2. Cage, qtd. in " 'Live' Electronic Music," 141.
3. Joseph Beuys, "Interview with Kate Horsefield," in *Joseph Beuys in America*, 71.
4. Joseph Beuys, " 'Death Keeps Me Awake': Interview with Achille Bonito-Oliva" (1986), in *Joseph Beuys in America*, 170.
5. Benjamin Buchloh's comments on Beuys's Free International University can be found in Buchloh's "Beuys: The Twilight of the Idol—Preliminary Notes for a Critique," *Artforum* 18.5 (Jan. 1980): 36. Buchloh's dismissal of Beuys's affirmation appears in Benjamin H. D. Buchloh, Rosalind Krauss, and Annette Michelson, "Beuys at the Guggenheim," *October*, no. 12 (Spring 1980): 14. All subsequent references to the latter work appear in the text.
6. Buchloh, "Beuys: The Twilight," 38.
7. Buchloh, "Beuys: The Twilight," 39.
8. Joseph Beuys, "Interview with Louwrien Wijers" (1979), in *Joseph Beuys in America*, 242.

Jappe, Jameson, and the Concept of Utopia ❑

As Georg Jappe rather more perceptively argues, Beuys's mythological provocations are potentially far more functional than orthodox discursive precision. Pondering upon the relevance of Beuys's aspirations, Jappe acknowledges that "much of this may seem utopian" but nevertheless concludes,

> At present the concept of Utopia is the most powerful weapon against the all-pervading scientific view that the world is only what it happens to be. . . . It is only by taking today as one's viewpoint and establishing a new evolutionary perspective, one which has not been mapped out beforehand, that the possible is achieved. Utopia is judged by the extent to which it is the art of the possible.[1]

While Jappe explicitly defends both the utopian project in postmodern art, and Beuys's art in particular, B-effect theorists such as Buchloh and Jameson tend either to deny the validity of this impulse or else offer it the most tokenistic recognition. Jameson's catalog essay for the Boston ICA exhibition *Utopia Post Utopia* (1988) embarrassingly concludes:

> It should also be noted that one finds everywhere today—not least among artists and writers—something like an unacknowledged "party of Utopia": an underground party, whose numbers are difficult to determine, whose program remains unannounced and perhaps even unformulated, whose existence is unknown to the citizenry at large and to the authorities, but whose members seem to recognize one another by means of secret masonic signals. One even has the feeling that some of the present exhibitors may be among its adherents.[2]

Reading such lines one can only assume that extreme exposure to science fiction could have induced Jameson to caricature, marginalize, and misinterpret the subject of his essay as a secret society of strange, androidlike creatures invading America everywhere through an unknown, unformulated, unannounced, and unacknowledged conspiracy. While often as little known to the citizenry and to the authorities as many of Jameson's writings, the work and the aspirations of the postmodern avant-garde are widely known, formulated, announced, and acknowledged across the pages of a broad spectrum of mainstream and underground publications, including most of the pages of the *Utopia Post Utopia* catalog. A cuckoo in this particular nest, Jameson's final ponderings upon the postmodern "Party of Utopia" only serve to demonstrate the disparity between the B-effect theorist's prejudices and preconceptions and the specific practices and publications of the culture they claim to analyze.

Notes

1. Georg Jappe, "A Joseph Beuys Primer," *Studio International* 183.936 (Sept. 1971): 69.
2. Fredric Jameson, "Postmodernism and Utopia," in *Utopia Post Utopia* (Boston: ICA, 1988), 32.

Bense, Concrete Poetry, and the Dwindling of the Poetic Element ❏

Cage's anecdote concerning the way in which he *dehexed* the frightening presence of a tape machine in Milan by simply sitting down and drawing it is emblematic of the process by which almost all modes of innovative or evolutionary postmodern creativity have initially been obliged to dehex their materials, one way or another.[1]

The fortunes of concrete poetry, from a predominantly formal genre avoiding reference to existential issues to a highly versatile mode of verbal-visual expression accompanied and complemented by modes of high-tech sound poetry, performance poetry, and public language art, typify the ways in which the most vital variants of postmodern narrative successively integrate, interrogate, and invalidate the mythologies of the B-effect prior to investigating—and perhaps elaborating—more utopian creative values.

Surveying some of the general assumptions of concrete poetry and other related textual experiments in his article "Theory and Practice of Text" (1964), the German poet and aesthetician Max Bense emphasizes the predominantly compositional rather than existential qualities of work "much less interested in the external world of objects than in its own private world of language."[2] From Bense's perspective, concrete poetry presents "textual and linguistic events" within "the particular environmental system of one or more words" (21). Accordingly, Bense examines the words making up concrete poems as "topological equivalents," analyzing "their relationships to their neighbours (systems of environment)" and "their material (visual, vocal, verbal) function" rather than "their objective factual meaning" (21–22). Acknowledging that this materialistic, topological approach to language leads to "the dwindling of the poetic element," Bense suggests that his curiously unpoetic poetics "corresponds exactly to the dwindling of vital human existence which is unavoidable in any technological civilization" (22).

One could be forgiven for assuming that concrete poetry represents the last formal retreat for the dud poet or the existential recluse. Not surprisingly, perhaps, critics such as Jost Hermand, writing on "West German Painting in the 1950s," draw attention to the way in which a certain "fetishism of the material" (by which Hermand means art's "divesting itself of all ties to specific subject or genre-related motifs, thematizing only its material") led the artist to "free himself from the 'dirty' business of politics" and to make pronouncements about "the beauty of technical form, of geometric patterns or mathematically calculated planes, as if one were dealing with the drawing-board blueprints of an engineering office."[3] With this in mind, Hermand adds, "Max Bense is not the only one at that time who compared the artist with a technical designer who proceeds from the laboratory situation" (31).

Both in his discussion of the "Theory and Practice of Text" and in two earlier "Concrete Poetry" manifestos of 1956, Bense posits that the experimental text is of greater interest as a model of compositional togetherness rather than as "an intentional carrier of meaning."[4] More or less intuitively dehexing Bense's fatalistic acceptance of the apparently unavoidable dwindling of both poetic content and "vital human existence," other pioneer concrete poets have insisted that this genre may communicate meaning quite as effectively as conventional linear poetry. For example, Eugen Gomringer's classic manifesto "From Line to Constellation" (1954) optimistically defends concrete poetry's abbreviated, restricted forms of language on the

71

grounds that "restriction in the best sense—concentration and simplification—is the very essence of poetry."[5] Noting that "the new poem is simple and can be perceived visually as a whole as well as in its parts," Gomringer concludes that at its most effective, the concrete poem—or *constellation*—"is memorable and imprints itself upon the mind as a picture" (67).

Gomringer also adds: "It is a reality in itself and not a poem about something or other" (67). By contrast, his manifesto "The Poem as a Functional Object" (1960) suggests that "the purpose of reduced language is not the reduction of language itself but the achievement of greater flexibility and freedom of communication" in works "as easily understood as signs in airports" or other developments arising from "positively-defined thinking."[6]

Most interesting here is Gomringer's suggestion that concrete poetry's reduced, formalistic basis is perfectly compatible with "positively-defined" technology—a suggestion anticipating the electronic signboards used in the eighties by feminist language artists such as Jenny Holzer and Barbara Kruger.

Considered very generally, Bense's highly conceptual approach to extralinear language typifies the tendency of B-effect theory to throw the baby out with the bathwater. Concrete poets such as the Scotsman Ian Hamilton Finlay and feminist language artists such as Holzer and Kruger have used compressed, extralinear texts—and compressed linear texts—to make some of the most idealistic, ethical statements and some of the most scathing, satirical comments of the eighties in response to complacent acceptance of the so-called "dwindling" of vital human existence within technological civilization.

Notes

1. Cage and Kostelanetz, "A Conversation about Radio," 21.

2. Max Bense, "Theory and Practice of Text" (1964), in *Astronauts of Inner Space: An International Collection of Avant-Garde Activity*, ed. Jeff Berner (San Francisco: Stolen Paper Editions, 1966), 20. All subsequent references to this article appear in the text.

3. Jost Hermand, "West German Painting in the 1950s," trans. Biddy Martin, *New German Critique*, no. 32 (Spring/Sum-

mer 1984): 30–31. All subsequent references to this article appear in the text.

4. Max Bense, "Concrete Poetry" (1965), trans. Irene Montjoye Sinor, *Hispanic Arts* 1.3–4 (Winter/Spring 1968): 73.

5. Eugen Gomringer, "From Line to Constellation" (1954), trans. Mike Weaver, *Hispanic Arts* 1.3–4 (Winter/Spring 1968): 67. All subsequent references to this article appear in the text.

6. Eugen Gomringer, "The Poem as a Functional Object," trans. Irene Montjoye Sinor, *Hispanic Arts* 1.3–4 (Winter/Spring 1968): 69–70.

Chopin, Human Vitality, and Technological Civilization ❑

Just as concrete poetry and electronic language art offers the modernist avant-garde's experiments with words-in-liberty systematic typographic, conceptual, and technological consolidation and extension, the predominantly abstract sound poetry experiments of Henri Chopin, François Dufrêne, and Isidore Isou and the predominantly semantic sound poetry experiments of Paul de Vree, Brion Gysin, Sten Hanson, Bernard Heidsieck, Ernst Jandl, Chris Mann, and Larry Wendt have equally systematically consolidated and extended the potential of the modernist avant-garde's phonetic, abstract, and simultaneous poems. Collectively, the research of such text-sound artists inaugurates a new, quintessentially postmodern technological tradition of sound art culminating in such recent public multimedia performances as Robert Ashley's, Charles Amirkhanian's, and Laurie Anderson's syntheses of *prerecorded, live,* and *real-time* manipulations of image, gesture, vocalic and nonvocalic sound.

Dehexing Bense's worst fears regarding language and the human spirit, the French poet Henri Chopin's early manifesto "Why I Am the Author of Sound Poetry and Free Poetry" (1967) characteristically asserts creative autonomy and rejects "the order imposed by the Word" in favor of sound poetry born of "the mimetic sound of man, the human sound," recorded, orchestrated, and generally transmuted by the technologies of the sixties.[1]

Confirming John Cage's suggestion in "Experimental Music" (1955) that "magnetic tape opens the door" and introduces "the unknown with such sharp clarity that anyone has the opportunity of having his habits blown away like dust" (*Silence*, 17), Chopin's "Open Letter to Aphonic Musicians" (1967) celebrates the ways in which "sound poetry, made for and by the tape-recorder," reveals how "the electronic means at our disposal give the word a new start and, at all events, disclose what, in the word, was a mere virtuality yesterday" (11, 22). Insisting, like Cage, that the artist can and must overcome fear of technology, Chopin confidently concludes, "Of course, for us electronics is simply a relaying of expression and by no means a master commanding our work" (22).

If Joseph Beuys's art and actions constitute what we may now think of as one of the most intelligent and vital manifestations of the *primitive* or *anthropological* impulse in radical postmodern culture, Chopin's research with sound poetry—or *audio-poésie*—like Cage's research with multimedia theater, typifies the most intelligent and vital *futuristic* or *technological* creative impulse of the sixties.

Chopin's particular achievements are best summarized by one of his peers, the Swedish sound poet and composer, Sten Hanson. Hanson argues that sound poetry is not so much an extension of futurist and dada experimentation as "a result of new working tools and new media: the tape-recorder, the electronic music studio, the L.P. record, the radio."[2] Acknowledging that Chopin was not "the very first poet" to use the tape recorder, Hanson suggests that he was certainly "the first to realize the fundamentally different possibilities it gave the oral poet" in the fifties; that he was "the first to make this theory clear"; and that he was "the first really important—and for ten years the only—regular publisher of sound poetry on records in his review *OU*" ("Henri Chopin," 16).

Chronicling Chopin's subsequent research with superimpressions and with multitrack spatialization of words, word fragments, and sound, Hanson concludes that Chopin's creative fusions of "the exactness of literature and the time manipulation of music . . . penetrate and influence the listener more deeply and more strongly than any other artistic method" (16). Like Beuys, Chopin's work suggests fundamental experiences and emotions through startlingly direct and startlingly simple means. Whereas Beuys employed elementary symbols such as his monumental wedges of fat, Chopin uses equally immediate sequences of elementary sounds in compositions such as *La Peur* (1971), a "40-minute poem about how man mobilizes all his inner resources to analyze and fight his fear— of destruction, of living, of dying" and thus, as Hanson puts it, "a poem about the best in human nature" ("Henri Chopin," 16).

Notes

1. Henri Chopin, "Why I Am the Author of Sound Poetry and Free Poetry" (1967), trans. Irene Montjoye Sinor, *Hispanic Arts* 1.3–4 (Winter/Spring 1968): 80–81.
2. Sten Hanson, "Henri Chopin, the Sound Poet," *Stereo Headphones*, no. 8-9-10 (1982): 16. All subsequent references to this article appear in the text.

Conz and the New Saints of the Avant-Garde ❏

In their different ways, Beuys, Chopin, and Cage all share the distinction of making highly significant initiatives within and across their media. Like other senior artists of their generation, they reconcile elements of inspired farce, elements of deep moral seriousness, and a spirit of highly independent confidence and innovation prompted, no doubt, by the difficulties of surviving several decades of public and critical indifference. While it may be true, as Max Bense suggests, in "Theory and Practice of Text," that vital human existence frequently seems in short supply among postmodern culture's mass audiences and institutional minders, it is certainly evident—notwithstanding Buchloh's arguments to the contrary—that many of the most interesting and innovative contemporary artists have been forced into the role of the "unique individual operating within an avant-garde tradition" (16).

However romantic the following hypothesis may appear, perhaps it is really the case, as the Italian publisher Francesco Conz surmises, that such avant-garde postmodern innovators are the "new saints," in the sense that they have often made "renunciations . . . as radical as the ones that were made by St. Francis in the thirteenth century."[1] In Conz's terms,

> instead of going into a convent and thinking about God, the modern way of looking for a spiritual life is much more a question of a private dedication to reading certain books and thinking certain thoughts and being involved in certain processes that are right at the center of avant-garde art. (Martin, "Conversation with Conz," 112)

Appraising the last quarter century's verbal-visual avant-garde, Conz concludes:

> We're talking about people who've had something important to say about our whole way of life, people who've raised some very radical objections and shown a dedication to a different kind of consciousness, a different awareness (113).

Note

1. Henry Martin, "A Conversation with Francesco Conz," *Lund Art Press* 2.2 (1991): 113. All subsequent references to this interview appear in the text.

A Problem in Design: Lax and Mann ❏

As Georg Jappe intimates in his appraisal of Beuys's utopian enthusiasms and as Francesco Conz confirms in his comments upon the avant-garde, innovative art has the particular conceptual advantage of supplementing prevailing definitions of what the world "happens to be" with new evolutionary perspectives revealing additional facets of "the art of the possible."[1]

The significance of utopian or avant-garde art might therefore be likened to that of an evolutionary or revolutionary spanner in the workings of what Jameson lucidly likens to overrationalized cultural theory's "increasingly closed and terrifying machine."[2] Predictably, the avant-garde's *open* gestures and assertions strike the increasingly closed and increasingly terrifying B-effect theorist as "simple-minded utopian drivel."[3]

Yet as Jameson himself admits in his essay "Reading Without Interpretation: Postmodernism and the Video-text" (1987), hard-line B-effect exegesis affords bitter rewards. Having systematically applied reductive intertextual theory to video art in order to demonstrate that "there are no video masterpieces," that "there can never be a video canon," and that "even an auteur theory of video . . . becomes very problematic indeed," since "the deepest 'subject' of all video art, and even of all postmodernism, is very precisely reproductive technology itself,"[4] Jameson gloomily concedes that he has simply leveled all video art—and all postmodern creativity—out of recognition. For according to his reasoning, "If all video-texts simply designate the process of production/reproduction, then presumably they all turn out to be 'the same' in a peculiarly unhelpful way" (222).

Max Bense's meticulous analysis, in "Theory and Practice of Text," of the structure and production of texts in terms of "a set of basic word events" accounting for "all potential texts" (21) takes a similarly unhelpful turn when it rather unexpectedly culminates in his supposition that human and textual vitality all turn out to be dwindling in the same unavoidable way.

Recommending Eric Satie's dictum, "Show me something new and I'll begin all over again," Cage helpfully emphasizes the ways in which the most vital avant-garde art provokes unavoidable *renewal*.[5] While the multimedia research of artists like Cage, Chopin, and Paik point to possibilities of *technological* innovation, poets such as the American Robert Lax and the Australian Chris Mann typify the *conceptual* innovation that Conz associates with "dedication to a different kind of consciousness."

Lax's work is best introduced in the context of Bense's notion of the poet and artist as textual engineer. Offering the perfect antidote to Bense's sense of the incompatibility between "exact conceptual and mathematical definition" (21) and the "poetic element" (22), Lax responds to "A Problem in Design" in the following way:

what if
you like
to draw
big flowers,

but what
if some
sage has
told you
that
there is

nothing
more
beautiful

nothing
more
beautiful

than a
straight
line
?

what should
you draw:
big flowers?
straight lines?

                    i think
                    you should
                    draw

                    big flowers
                    big flowers

                    big flowers
                    big flowers

                    big flowers
                    big flowers

                    big flowers
                    big flowers

                    until
                    they become
                    a straight
                    line.[6]

Lax's solution to the problem of combining images of big flowers and straight lines serves both as a general demonstration of the compatibility between structural and subjective poetics and as a more specific index of the way in which his own partially minimalist, partially concrete, partially abstract, and partially devotional practice effortlessly combines surprisingly formal orchestrations of sound, sign, and meaning (along the vertical axis of his stanzas' *straight line*) with highly personal, immediately accessible, existential insights.

The Australian poet Chris Mann rather similarly deflates the more dogmatic assumptions of linguistics and philosophy in the highly crafted monologue pieces that Cage annunciates as "a new direction in poetry."[7] Mixing cryptic assertion and anecdotal anti-assertion, one of the most powerful sections of Mann's "SCRATCH SCRATCH" begins:

1. CHOMSKY WAS AN EARLY NATO SET-UP.

2. CREDIT IS DISTRACTION FORMALIZED. ALL I KNOW ABOUT MORGENBESSER IS THE ONE THAT GOES THAT THERE WAS THIS LADY PHILOSOPHER ADDRESSING A BUNCH OF PHILOSOPHERS ON THE DISTINCTIONS BETWEEN ARTIFICIAL AND NATURAL LANGUAGES & SHE WAS GOING ON THAT ALL THE LANGUAGES SHE KNEW—WHETHER ARTIFICIAL OR NATURAL

LANGUAGES—THAT IN ALL THESE LANGUAGES A
DOUBLE NEGATIVE ALWAYS MEANS A POSITIVE BUT
THAT SHE KNEW OF NO LANGUAGE EITHER NATURAL
OR ARTIFICIAL WHERE A DOUBLE POSITIVE MEANT
ANYTHING BUT A POSITIVE, WHEREUPON
MORGENBESSER IS HEARD TO PIPE UP FROM THE
BACK, YEAH YEAH[8]

Delivered at racetrack commentary speed, in a consciously exaggerated Australian accent, Mann's work is at once an assertion of the possibility of a distinctly Australian grammar, a commentary upon wide-ranging theoretical, musical, historical, economical, and ethical orthodoxies, and in performative terms an extremely amusing and inventive mode of narration. Criticized for reading too fast, Mann is apt to criticize his audiences for listening "too slow." Robert Lax's performances, by contrast tend to be both slow and solemn; indeed, Lax relates that members of his audience report that they breathe more restfully during his readings.

Irrespective of their differences, both Lax and Mann exemplify the way in which independent researchers have synthesized the structural thematic and performative potential of postmodern writing in highly original, highly amusing, and highly referential formal experiments demonstrating the possible continuity, contemporaneity, and compatibility of all the textual and authorial energies that Bense and Gomringer associate with—or dissociate from—"the very essence of poetry" (Gomringer, "From Line," 67).

Notes

1. Jappe, "A Joseph Beuys Primer," 69.
2. Jameson, "Postmodernism, or the Cultural Logic," 57.
3. Buchloh, "Beuys: The Twilight," 36.
4. Fredric Jameson "Reading Without Interpretation: Postmodernism and the Video-Text" (1987), in *The Linguistics of Writing: Arguments Between Language and Literature*, ed. Nigel Fabb, Derek Attridge, Alan Durant, and Colin MacCabe (Manchester, Eng.: Manchester Univ. Press, 1987), 208–209. All subsequent page references to this article appear in the text.
5. Cage, *Eyeline*, 6.

6. Robert Lax, "A Problem in Design," in *33 Poems*, by Lax, ed. Thomas Kellein (Stuttgart: Edition Hansjorg Mayer, 1987), 144.

7. Cage, *Eyeline*, 6.

8. Chris Mann, "SCRATCH SCRATCH," in *Off the Record*, ed. Pi O (Ringwood, Australia: Penguin, 1985), 105.

Postmodernism at Two Speeds: Hassan, Janco, and Seuphor ❑

Bense's and Lax's different responses to postmodern poetry's "Problem in Design" usefully illustrate the plurality and the ambiguity of the postmodern temper. While both Bense and Lax display enthusiasm for minimal language art—an international avant-garde that first flourished as a self-conscious multimedia movement in the sixties and seventies—their respective approaches to language art clearly diverge in terms of the antithetical categories that Ihab Hassan might designate as *purpose* and *play, design* and *chance, absence* and *presence.*[1] While Bense's topological aesthetic virtually accepts the elimination of authorial presence, Lax proposes the cheerful coexistence of purpose, design, play, chance, and authorial enthusiasm for big flowers.

At different times and to differing degrees, other postmodern writers, performers, and composers—such as the French "new" novelist Alain Robbe-Grillet, the American dancer and filmmaker Yvonne Rainer, and the American composer Steve Reich—evince similar tensions and transitions between the conflicting claims of structural anonymity and confessional subjectivity, formal neutrality and existential sensitivity.

Discussing Yvonne Rainer's film *The Man Who Envied Women* (1985), Patricia Mellencamp describes it as "a bold move toward a new scenario—women's subjectivity."[2] Applauding Rainer's send-up of one pretentious male "masquerading as a feminist—in theoretical drag" (*Indiscretions*, 177), Mellencamp emphasizes Rainer's general satire of the way in which "theory

. . . is migrating and being commodified as fodder for the art world as well as academia . . . [as] . . . passwords for exchange and seduction," becoming at worst "a hobby that is 'done' (I 'do' theory)" (182).

In a sense, a great many artists could have claimed to *do* structuralist theory in the sixties, whereas in the late eighties and early nineties they might claim to *do* subjectivity, biography, or history. What becomes evident from such transitions, perhaps, is that it makes little sense anymore to attempt to distinguish postmodern creativity from modernism in terms of schematic oppositions, such as the following distinctions taken from Ihab Hassan's list of "differences" in his essay "Toward a Concept of Postmodernism" (1982).

Modernism	Postmodernism
Romanticism/Symbolism	Pataphysics/Dadaism
Form (conjunctive, closed)	Antiform (disjunctive, open)
Purpose	Play
Design	Chance
Hierarchy	Anarchy
Mastery/Logos	Exhaustion/Silence
Art object/Finished work	Decreation/Deconstruction.[3]

As the successive phases and internal contradictions of postmodern culture become more explicit, it appears increasingly obvious that the terms juxtaposed in Hassan's schema are not so much peculiar to modernism or postmodernism as they are examples of tensions common to both of these different eras. Modernist culture is continually animated by the tension between the romantic/symbolist impulse and the pataphysical/ dadaist impulse; and the suggestion that pataphysical and dadaist poetics are somehow exclusively postmodern is both historically and empirically confusing.

It is probably more helpful to acknowledge that certain *phases* of modernist culture evince a more or less dominant symbolist or dadaist poetics, just as certain *phases* of postmodern culture evince and extend these poetics in different ways some forty or fifty years later. For every postmodern exponent of play, chance, and anarchy, there is a modernist precursor.

Likewise, for every modernist artist preoccupied with purpose, design, and hierarchy, there are postmodern successors.

Reassessing dadaism's contradictions in his article "Dada at Two Speeds" (1966), the veteran Zurich dadaist, Marcel Janco, emphasizes the ways in which dada's notorious initial "scandalous force" and "irrational attacks" gradually changed course as certain dada artists went "beyond the first speed, the negative speed" and affirmed "a new creative route."[4] Regretfully acknowledging that the "spiritual violence of the first phase . . . impressed minds and imprinted a stamp which could not be effaced," Janco noted that even in the mid-sixties, people were "surprised to find that the best Dadas, like Jean Arp, seem least Dada" (37).

The best postmodern artists, such as Cage and Beuys, similarly seem *least* postmodern when judged in terms of the monodimensional mythologies contributing to postmodern culture's early reputation. Impressed by the scandalous force of Cage's and Beuys's early gestures and writings and by the seductive negative speed of B-effect theory, critical attention has tended to overlook the "new creative routes" inaugurated by these artists.

With the benefit of historical hindsight, Janco responded more perceptively to postmodern culture's positive speed, declaring himself to be "astounded . . . by the fantastic mechanical and technological progress" informing the new poetry of those postmoderns successfully experimenting with "radio-waves, stereo, the tape-recorder."[5]

The art critic and poet Michel Seuphor complements Janco's analysis of modernism's positive and negative impulses with analysis of the more thematic tension between commitment to the poles of "style and cry, rule and outburst."[6] Identical antitheses animate the phases of postmodern creativity.

In such circumstances, one of the most interesting challenges for the cultural historian and cultural cartographer is the task of delineating the specific ways in which modern and postmodern artists, writers, and theorists represent and respond to the polarities of purpose and play, design and chance, style and cry.

One might argue, perhaps, that the concrete and visual poetry movements of the sixties and seventies offered extralinear language far more systematic geometric and metaphoric orchestration than the early typographic experiments of dada and futurism and that the recording technologies of the sixties, seventies, and eighties allowed poets and artists to *identify, superimpose,* and *orchestrate* fragments of sound and image with a degree of precision unknown to modernist collagists and sound poets such as Raoul Hausmann and Kurt Schwitters. Both technologically and conceptually, postmodern verbal-visual creativity is considerably more sophisticated and informed than its modernist precursors. As Henri Chopin suggests in a letter contrasting the avant-gardes of the early and late twentieth century in aviational terms, "the plane piloted by Blériot cannot be compared with supersonic planes like the Concorde."[7]

Ihab Hassan's early typological distinctions between modernism and postmodernism set up rather misleading contrasts between these eras' supposedly mutually exclusive priorities. As these pages have argued, it seems more productive to acknowledge that the quite different cultural, social, and technological climates of modernism and postmodernism both often address—and at times resolve—identical contradictions. Hassan's recent essay "Making Sense: The Trials of Postmodern Discourse" (1987) helpfully diagnoses the ways in which the late postmodern temper tends to reconcile several conflicting priorities. Affirming Yves Bonnefoy's sense that the time is right for "a re-turn to being or presence," "a reflux of language to human relations," Hassan identifies the eighties as a time for "provisional reconstructions, pragmatic remythifications."[8]

For several decades, this impulse towards reconstruction, remythification, and the assertion of presence has consistently informed the *positive speed* of such visionary postmoderns as Cage, Lax, and Beuys. What seems particularly significant in the eighties is the way in which other artists previously caught up in the *negative speed* of the structuralist sixties have subsequently revised their values in order to address the wider issues and languages of human relations. Surprisingly, perhaps, the eighties witness a major collective, chronological, conceptual shift, reasserting and reaffirming precisely those aspects of personal and social identity to which postmoderns such as Robbe-Grillet, Rainer, and Reich once seemed most vehemently opposed.

Notes

1. Ihab Hassan, *The Postmodern Turn: Essays on Postmodern Theory and Culture* (Ohio: Ohio State Univ. Press, 1987), 91.
2. Patricia Mellencamp, *Indiscretions: Avant-Garde Film, Video and Feminism* (Bloomington: Indiana Univ. Press, 1990), 173. All subsequent references to this work appear in the text.
3. Ihab Hassan, "Toward a Concept of Modernism," in *The Postmodern Turn*, 91.
4. Marcel Janco, "Dada at Two Speeds" (1966), in *Dadas on Art*, ed. Lucy Lippard (Englewood Cliffs, N.J.: Prentice-Hall, 1971), 36–37. All subsequent references to this article appear in the text.
5. Marcel Janco, letter, 1 Aug. 1979, *Stereo Headphones*, no. 8-9-10 (1982): 75. My translation.
6. Michel Seuphor, *La peinture abstraite* (Paris: Flammarion, 1964), 62. My translation.
7. Henri Chopin, letter, 17 July 1979, *Stereo Headphones*, no. 8-9-10 (1982): 74. My translation.
8. Hassan refers here to Bonnefoy's "Image and History: Yves Bonnefoy's Inaugural Address at the Collège de France," *New Literary History* 15.3 (Spring 1984): 447. The quote by Hassan is from *The Postmodern Turn*, 204.

Rainer, Robbe-Grillet, Reich, and the Turn to Interobjectivity ❑

The resurgence of the "human" element in the work of Rainer, Robbe-Grillet, and Reich is best defined in terms of the contrasts between their writings of the sixties and subsequent accounts of their works in the eighties. Yvonne Rainer's early essay, "A Quasi Survey of Some 'Minimalist' Tendencies in the Quantitatively Minimal Dance Activity Midst the Plethora, or an Analysis of *Trio A*" (1968), discerningly traces the ways in which her own dances and the minimalist sculptures of the sixties promulgated a "self-contained" and "objectlike" aesthetic.[1]

Virtually excluding personal expression and specialized technique, her approach to dance emphasized processes of neutral action on the assumption that "action, or what one does, is more interesting and important than the exhibition of character and attitude, and that action can best be focussed on through the submerging of the personality; so ideally one is not even oneself, one is a neutral 'doer.' " Accordingly, Rainer attempted to present "a more matter-of-fact, more concrete, more banal quality of physical being in performance" (267).

Positing that minimal sculpture aimed to eliminate or minimize the "role of artist's hand," figure reference, and illusionism, just as her dances rejected phrasing, character, and performance, Rainer listed possible alternative priorities in the following diagrammatic summary:

Objects	Dances
1. factory fabrication	energy equality and "found" movement
2. unitary forms, modules	equality of parts
3. uninterrupted surface	repetition of discrete events
4. nonreferential forms	neutral performance
5. literalness	task or tasklike activity
6. simplicity	singular action, event, or tone

(263)

Writing in *For a New Novel* (1965), Alain Robbe-Grillet called for the similarly nonreferential, literal, and tasklike fiction that he rather ambiguously defined as an " 'inhuman' work" in which the protagonist's eyes would "rest on things without indulgence."[2] Accordingly,

he sees them, but he refuses to appropriate them, he refuses to maintain any suspect understanding with them, any complicity; he asks nothing of them . . . his sense of sight is content to take their measurements; and his passion, similarly, rests on their surface, without attempting to penetrate them since there is nothing inside, without feigning the least appeal since they would not answer. (98)

The proximity between Robbe-Grillet's ideals and those of Barthes's essay "The Death of the Author" is obvious. Like Robbe-Grillet, Barthes proposes that critics should simply take the "measurements" of writing, without attempting to penetrate its surface. Writing, Barthes proposes, allows "everything . . . to be *disentangled*, but nothing *deciphered*." It follows then, that "the space of writing is to be traversed, not pierced."[3]

Not surprisingly, Barthes championed Robbe-Grillet's fiction as "the exact opposite of poetic writing," claiming that such fiction "has no alibi, no density, and no depth: it remains on the surface of the object and inspects it impartially."[4] At most, Robbe-Grillet's language apparently serves simply "to 'paint' the object . . . to deposit little by little in the circuit of its space an entire chain of gradual names, none of which will exhaust it" ("Objective Literature," 14).

Steve Reich's essay "Music as a Gradual Process" (1968) adumbrates a similarly impartial and gradual compositional ideal, describing what Barthes might have termed the *pleasure* of disentangling structural continuity or what Rainer might describe as the *neutral* repetition of impersonal events. Observing that Cage's musical parameters "can't be heard" clearly in performance, Reich proposes "a compositional process and a sounding music that are one and the same thing."[5]

In order to clarify this process in performance, Reich envisages compositions "happening extremely gradually," affording an experience somewhat like "watching a minute hand on a watch" (11). Just as Robbe-Grillet and Rainer envisage inhuman compositions submerging the personality, Reich predicts that the desired contemplation of "details of . . . sound . . . occurring for their own acoustic reasons" will provide "a particularly liberating and impersonal kind of ritual . . . [making] possible that shift of attention from *he* and *she* and *you* and *me* towards *it*" (11).

Collectively, Rainer's, Robbe-Grillet's, and Reich's manifestos of the sixties all give the impression that postmodern creativity is characterized by a curiously flat, neutral mode of *interobjectivity*.

Notes

1. Yvonne Rainer, "A Quasi Survey of Some 'Minimalist' Tendencies in the Quantitatively Minimal Dance Activity Midst the Plethora, or an Analysis of *Trio A*," in *Minimal Art: A Critical Anthology*, ed. Gregory Battcock (New York: E. P. Dutton, 1968), 271. All subsequent references to this article appear in the text.

2. Alain Robbe-Grillet, extracts from *For a New Novel* (1965), in *The Discontinuous Universe: Selected Writings in Contemporary Consciousness*, ed. Sallie Sears and Georgianna W. Lord (New York: Basic Books, 1972), 98. All subsequent references to this work appear in the text.

3. Barthes, "Death of the Author," 147.

4. Roland Barthes, "Objective Literature," in *Critical Essays* by Barthes, (Evanston: Northwestern Univ. Press, 1972), 14. All subsequent page references to this essay appear in the text.

5. Steve Reich, "Music as a Gradual Process" (1968), in *Writings about Music*, by Reich (Halifax, N.S.: Press of the Novia Scotia College of Art and Design, 1974): 10. All subsequent references to this essay appear in the text.

Robbe-Grillet and the Re-turn to the Subjective Type of Writing ❑

Unlike their writing of the sixties, Robbe-Grillet's, Rainer's, and Reich's more recent statements reflect what Hassan terms a *re-turn* to subjectivity and to the intersubjective languages of human relations.

Reassessing critical responses to his work in an interview of 1986, Robbe-Grillet repeatedly stressed the idiosyncratic and personal dimensions of his writing, as though its central traits were not so much clinical detachment and objectivity as lightly veiled authorial joviality. Alluding to the humor, the surrealism, the phantasmagoria, and the phantasms in his fiction, Robbe-Grillet confides: "I would describe the type of literature I write as a subjective type of writing, but geared to, projected towards an object."[1]

Implicitly discrediting the relevance of his own earlier references to his work's inhuman qualities and more or less explicitly denying the relevance of Barthes's emphases upon his work's antipoetic qualities, Robbe-Grillet adds, "What harmed the New Novel was not Barthes's views, but a simplification of what he had said, which reduced the whole impact to a bland, neutral, factual type of writing" ("Confessions," 10).

Like the supposedly naturalistic narratives of Emile Zola, Robbe-Grillet's pseudoscientific "new" novels are frequently subverted by the presence of such consciously phantasmagoric detail as his repeated descriptions of a centipede squashed into the shape of a question mark in *La Jalousie* (1957). Whether such studied exceptions to the prevailing tedium of his fiction justify its redefinition as humorous, as surreal, or as the kind of pop art fiction with which Robbe-Grillet now associates his work—when relating, "I deal with popular imagery . . . from a critical distancing point of view" ("Confessions," 11)—is another matter.

Baudrillard's *America* (1988) very interestingly speculates that while European intellectuals "are at home with . . . different effects of meaning coexisting under the umbrella of the concept," this very element of conceptual or critical distancing prevents them from emulating their American counterparts' capacity to evoke "the object freed from its concept . . . in extroverted form, in the equivalence of all its effects."[2]

Baudrillard's subsequent claim that unrestrained extroversion is a total enigma to the European mind is at least partially applicable to Robbe-Grillet's writing.[3] At best, Robbe-Grillet *rationalizes* his work's comic, surreal, or pop qualities rather than consistently manifesting these traits with any particular lightness of touch. As he suggests, it is perhaps in his cinematic work that his vision's phantasms become most explicit.

Notes

1. Alain Robbe-Grillet, "Confessions of a Voyeur," interview with Roland Caputo, *Tension* (Melbourne), no. 10 (1986): 10. All subsequent references to this interview appear in the text.

2. Jean Baudrillard, *America*, trans. Chris Turner (London: Verso, 1988), 99.

3. Baudrillard, *America*, 99.

Rainer and the Re-turn to Identity ❑

Like Robbe-Grillet, Yvonne Rainer seems to have required the catalyst of cinematic creativity to break away from her initial relatively austere poetics. Recollecting that Robbe-Grillet's *For a New Novel* was one of her "favourite books" in the mid-sixties, Rainer now acknowledges that her early minimalist dance manifesto growing out of *Parts of Some Sextets* was "totally overstated" in order to "clear the air and provoke."[1] More specifically, Rainer now emphasizes the ambivalence of her approach to the conventions of representation. Although her dance manifesto asserted "no to magic or make believe," Rainer explains, "I went into film which is certainly a kind of magic and illusion . . . because there was the opportunity for that extreme of illusion, but also the opportunity to probe it and to undermine it" (interview with author, 7 Feb. 1992).

While Rainer admits that her dance projects of the sixties involved "working with groups of people in unison, in formal designs" without "reference in dance to things outside of itself," her recent films focus quite systematically upon things outside of self-referential formal designs.[2] If Rainer's minimalist dances proposed that "virtuosic movement" and variety be replaced by "neutral performance" and "tasklike activity," films such as *The Man Who Envied Women* (1985) offer what Patricia Mellencamp describes in *Indiscretions* as "a technically brilliant and casual orchestration of bits of synched (and non) image and dialogue . . . picked up from performing passersby on New York streets . . . in a tour-de-force cacophony of Manhattan commentary and trends" (183).

As Mellencamp points out, Rainer's film juxtaposes "lifeless theory . . . yoked to the male body and voice" against "the wise kaleidoscope of women's voices, images, and issues which swirl like a whirligig through the film" (182), thereby challenging dominant "bleak" theories of " 'loss'—of narrative, the dominance or mastery of vision, personal stories of authors, and history" by asserting "culturally . . . and historically grounded" evidence (185).

Rainer's own address "Narrative in the (Dis)Service of Identity" (1990) repeatedly emphasizes her determination to assert identity, to "speak for myself," and "to use language and narrative in ways that are appropriate to specific struggles," even if this means returning to more conventional forms of narrative, "the better to break them."[3] As Rainer explains in the following rather extensive section from her address, her present practice marks a blend of both antinarrative and more traditional "narrative soup" in order to accommodate all the issues "outside of the art object" to which her film *Privilege* (1990) refers. Specifying that she is still using "the same strategies of narrative subversion" but has shifted slightly in relation to "certain cinematic conventions" with regard to "the matter of identification," Rainer relates:

> I was previously wary of being "swallowed up" in that process of identification which makes you feel you are one with the character you follow on the screen. . . . As my texts became more explicitly theoretical or political, however, I began to feel a greater obligation to assign their utterance to more unified identities, which traditionally accumulated their coherence via constant motion across a spacio-temporal field. A rather stilted way of saying Yikes! We're in the narrative soup once more. The devices of my earlier work—the impersonal narrator and what I shall call "character proxies," or mouth-pieces, constituted a refusal to invest my film performances with the stature and authority of full-blown characters. Finally, however, the sheer abundance of issues and ideas that I wanted to include in *Privilege* required more help from such characters. The spectator must be enabled to identify with situations—and characters are a large but not the only part of this process—in order to make connections to the world outside of the art object.[4]

Notes

1. Yvonne Rainer, interview with author, 7 Feb. 1992. All subsequent references to this interview appear in the text.
2. The quotes are from Yvonne Rainer, "Naming Myself," interview with Rachel Fensham and Jude Walton, *Writings on Dance*, no. 7 (1991): 12.
3. Yvonne Rainer, "Narrative in the (Dis)Service of Identity" (1990), *Agenda* (Melbourne), no. 17 (May 1991): 12, 14.
4. Rainer, "Narrative," 14.

Reich and the Re-turn to Historical Realities ❏

Like the recent films of Yvonne Rainer, the recent compositions of Steve Reich are characterized by the return to relatively conventional narrative and to an emphasis upon questions of personal, social, and national identity. Whereas Reich's notes on "Music as a Gradual Process" shifted attention to the *it* of details of sound—"away from *he* and *she* and *you* and *me*"— compositions such as *Different Trains* (1988) reverse this emphasis by requiring instruments to imitate the quite specific voice patterns of "my governess Virginia, now in her 70s, reminiscing about our train trips together"; of "a retired Pullman porter, Lawrence Davis, now in his 80s, who used to ride lines between New York and Los Angeles reminiscing about his life"; and of "Holocaust survivors Rachella, Paul and Rachel—all about my age and now living in America—speaking of their experiences."[1]

Combined with recordings of American and European train sounds from the thirties and forties, *Different Trains* is at once an autobiographical allusion to Reich's own childhood train journeys to his divorced parents in Los Angeles and New York; an exploration of the experiences of the "very different" train journeys of his Jewish contemporaries in Europe; a retrospective trans-Atlantic comparison of this "whole situation"; and compositionally, "a new way" of combining speech and sound samples (transferred to tape by computer) with live string quartet performance (Notes, *Different Trains*).

As Reich suggests, *Different Trains* is also a transitional work leading to the "new kind of documentary music video theatre" that he explores in his most recent and most ambitious multimedia project, *The Cave*. Discussing this work Reich specifies:

> *The Cave* is about the Cave of Machpelah, in the town of Hebron on the West Bank, where Abraham from the Bible is buried. And it is very much the roots of the situation in the Middle East today. The patriarch Abraham had two sons. One of them is Isaac who is the father of the Jewish people, and the other is Ishmael through Hagar, Sarah's slave girl, who is the acknowledged progenitor of the Arabs. So in essence, you have here a kind of family paradigm for the roots of a conflict which . . . began in the Biblical period, and was brought to a boil with the writing of the Koran in the sixth century.[2]

Arguing that the contemporary Middle East conflict can only be clearly understood in terms of such historical realities, Reich proposes to combine video and audio sampling of "real live human beings living in that part of the world, who get a chance to comment on simple questions like 'Who for you is Abraham?,' 'Who for you is Isaac?' . . . 'Who for you is Ishmael?' " within the musical context of "the melodies of voices doubled by musicians and singers" (interview with author, 12 Mar. 1990).

Like Rainer's films, Reich's "documentary music video theatre" is consciously culturally, historically, and locally grounded: three traits which—as Patricia Mellencamp observes in *Indiscretions*—refreshingly counteract fashionable mythologies of assorted cultural and conceptual "loss" (185).

Notes

1. Steve Reich, notes to *Different Trains* (Elektra/Nonesuch, 1989), sound recording. All of Reich's references to *Different Trains* are taken from these notes and appear in the text.

2. Steve Reich, interview with author, 12 Mar. 1990. All of Reich's references to *The Cave* are taken from this interview and appear in the text.

Multimedia Art in the Age of Mechanical Reproduction: Gaburo and Ashley ❏

As Steve Reich pragmatically speculates, documentary music video theater performances such as *The Cave* are likely to have "virtually no political effect" just as Kurt Weill's music had no effect on Hitler other than placing Weill in a situation in which he had to "run like hell" (interview with author, 12 Mar. 1990). Reich's reservations are almost certainly compounded by his sense of the limited public accessibility awaiting expensive multimedia productions.

Reich's fellow composer Kenneth Gaburo still more bluntly comments, "I frankly don't know what an audience is, so I can't possibly imagine writing for one."[1] Like Reich's and Rainer's most recent works, Gaburo's work-in-progress, *Testimony*, incorporates quite specific fragments of public dialogue in order to create "a kind of oral history on the topic of nuclear war" based upon responses to the question: "In the event of a nuclear war, humans would be sacrificed. This sacrifice could not take place unless human life was thought to be expendable. In this, your life is included. How do you feel about being expendable?" (interview with author, 5 Nov. 1990).

As Gaburo indicates, the sociopolitical concerns of *Testimony* led him to explore an unusual variant of interactive video art requiring "individuals—one at a time—to respond as they please to this question, before a fixed video camera" as it is read "off-camera—usually by the person who has just completed a testimony." Subsequently, *Testimony* extended into the realm of interactive radio art, when "Andrew McLennan of ABC Radio in Australia asked if it was possible to have a call-in response to the question, to be aired on Hiroshima Day" (interview with author, 5 Nov. 1990).

Gaburo's enthusiasm for the ABC's "fantastic" radio version of *Testimony* and his proposal to present the final version of its "massive four space act theatre, based on the subject of war-making, male-sexuality, violence, and the social nature of argu-

94

ment," both as an initial installation and as an eventual "two-hour broadcast-quality tape," make it clear that despite his basic doubts about audiences, he certainly envisages that *Testimony* might receive some sort of public attention, either as multimedia installation art or as privately or publicly screened video art (interview with author, 5 Nov. 1990).

Gaburo's *Testimony* project pinpoints the ways in which many of the most imaginative and socially and politically sensitive postmodern multimedia artists regard new recording and reproductive technologies not so much as what Jameson calls "a structure or sign-flow which resists meaning" as a structure or sign-flow that facilitates public impact and interaction.

Optimistically appraising the technologies utilized by sound poets, Henri Chopin comments, "we have with mass media and radio the ability to be heard around the world by everyone . . . all you need is to produce an edition of fifty cassettes."[2] Chopin obviously refers here to the international network of avant-garde poets, critics—and most significantly—radio producers, such as the ABC's Andrew McLennan, KPFA's Charles Amirkhanian, ORF's Heidi Grundmann, and WDR's Klaus Schöning, whose collective efforts frequently allow the most recent sound art experiments to be "heard around the world by everyone."

Nevertheless, as the American composer Robert Ashley recounts, opportunities to broadcast television variants of such multimedia work, such as the half-hour episodes of his opera *Perfect Lives* made in collaboration with England's channel four, are few and far between. Each episode was to be made as seven synchronic tapes, and Ashley envisaged that a range of television stations would subsequently rebroadcast *Perfect Lives* as an alternative, real-time, mass-media performance piece, by resynchronizing the seven tapes for each episode as though they were "the seven replay tapes of a sporting event." But as Ashley admits, he was finally discouraged by mass culture's "practical necessities."

> From talking to people I realized that the technique was real, but was unavailable. In other words, you really could do all this synchronization thing, because you could see it on the most expensive sporting events—fourteen cameras, six replays, five

graphic inputs and this sort of stuff. So naturally, that's what you dream about. It was not visionary from a technical point of view, but it was visionary from a financial point of view. . . . I didn't realize that there might be such a financial barrier, or aesthetic barrier, or barrier of the imagination.[3]

Subsequently marketing videotape versions of his operas, Ashley enthusiastically describes this initiative as "the most successful thing that could have happened to me," adding,

What I'm happy about—and what I predicted—is that people really want the videotapes . . . they're distributed by independent distributors—not so much the stores, which are all very new, and which are still dominated by the beginning attempt at mass-market saturation. (interview with author, 12 Jan. 1991)

Just as Cage describes his multimedia experiments as "a form of theatre with which I'm unfamiliar,"[4] which he looks forward to experiencing, Ashley movingly articulates his wish to continue his work with television opera in terms of his desire both to become experientially wiser about this genre and his wish to realize utopian projects that he knows to be possible:

I hope that I'll be able to finish this large project that I've set out for myself, because I'd like to be able to see it myself. If I could make thirty-nine or forty half-hour episodes, and be able to look at those as a piece, I would be a lot wiser than I am right now about talking about television and that kind of stuff. In other words, I'm still in the position, unfortunately, of being the visionary—of advocating something that is outside of my experience. But I know that it's possible. (interview with author, 12 Jan. 1991)

Referring in turn to the "very tricky" conjunction of independent creativity and independent distribution, Yvonne Rainer equally affirmatively concludes,

People ask me, "Are you ever going to make a real movie?" because real movies get larger numbers of people. But I do things in my movies that I couldn't do in "real movies" and over a period of time the numbers of people who will have seen my films will be vast. They keep getting shown and small audiences occur in many different places.[5]

Artists like Rainer, Reich, Gaburo, Chopin, and Ashley command considerable respect for continuing the positive avant-garde tradition of working outside and against the financial barrier, the aesthetic barrier, and the barrier of the imagination that condition prevailing cultural and critical expectations. Variously reaffirming the kind of aesthetic and sociopolitical values that Jameson eccentrically believes that "it was in the revolutionary nature of the newer medium to have precisely effaced and dispelled" ("Reading Without Interpretation," 209), the work of these artists demonstrates that despite the overwhelming vulgarity and frivolity of popular, mass-market media culture, the newer media are most significant as the evolutionary source of profoundly new creative practices and possibilities.

Notes

1. Kenneth Gaburo, interview with author, 5 Nov. 1990. All subsequent references to this interview appear in the text.
2. Henri Chopin, interview with Lawrence Kucharz, Larry Wendt, and Ellen Zweig (1978), *Stereo Headphones*, no. 8-9-10 (1982): 13.
3. Robert Ashley, interview with the author, 12 Jan. 1991. All subsequent references to this interview appear in the text.
4. Cage, *Eyeline*, 6.
5. Yvonne Rainer, "Naming Myself," 20.

Monk and the Re-turn to Recurrence ❑

Remarking upon the difference between her own creativity and the multimedia performances of the New York singer, dancer, and choreographer Meredith Monk, Yvonne Rainer observes that whereas her own successive films have focused upon "specific, topical issues," "Meredith is working with what she sees as essences" (interview with author, 7 Feb. 1992). Monk in turn explains that her art attempts to emphasize certain recurrent continuities within the apparently fragmented mosaic of contemporary experience.

> Whereas the European tradition was very much about separating elements and devoting one's life to being a specialist, I think you could say that the world we live in now is much more of a mosaic way of perceiving. To me it seems important to do an artform which reflects that—and then also, in a sense, to give the opportunity to the members of the audience to sense the fullness of their experience and the fullness of all the aspects of themselves. ... I'm interested in ... things that have always been in the world and always will be. So just by the nature of that, it already does imply a different kind of spiralic layer to that mosaic—it's still mosaic, but there's also a spiral within that.[1]

Characterizing her performances as attempts to synthesize past and present sensibilities, Monk suggests, "It's like affirming roots in the past, in order to be able to live fully in the present" (interview with author, 5 Feb. 1992). Considered more generally, Monk's "spiralic" aesthetic offers a helpful conceptual bridge, linking the technological impulse within postmodern culture with its concurrent—and not necessarily incompatible—retrospective impulse. Significantly, Monk argues that her work comfortably encompasses both domains, in the interest of creative flexibility.

> I don't have a very strong attitude about it one way or the other. You use technology when you use it for what it can do. I certainly sing in front of a microphone and I use lights, although I also feel that I'd be very comfortable singing with one candle. . . . Basically I think that what we need to do now, all of us—as human beings and as artists—is just to learn how to be incredibly flexible. I think that's why the hard times in a sense are kind of interesting—because I feel that's what they're calling upon us to do—to be very fluid and very flexible with what comes up. (interview with author, 5 Feb. 1992)

Monk's response to the counterproductive excesses of the mass media are both lucid and pragmatic. Commenting upon the velocity of children's television, Monk remarks, "The level of bombardment and speed is so overwhelming that you realize that they're being taught to not be involved . . . they're taught to read images quickly . . . every image is equal to every other image . . . [and] . . . discriminating intelligence gets atrophied." With this problem in mind, Monk argues that "one of the reasons for doing art now is to have the antidote to numbing" and concludes:

> At the risk of sounding corny, I would say that I do have a very strong belief in the art process as a healing process, and that it's very necessary in the world we live in now that there's some place where people can actually experience alternative ways of behaviour—in terms of the people that are performing and what's being performed . . . so that they would want to have that quality of life and wouldn't stand for less. (interview with author, 5 Feb. 1992)

Monk's capacity to work concurrently with and between high and low technologies, ranging from complex multimedia operas like *Atlas* (1991) to more economical, simple productions like *Facing North* (1990), typifies the wider, more positive parameters of postmodern culture. As Monk suggests, many aspects of historically and technologically postmodern culture share an essential continuity with previous eras despite their distinctively different cultural context. "I feel that what I'm doing is not so different from . . . what artists in the twenties or thirties or forties were doing. . . . I'm just doing it in my own way" (interview with author, 5 Feb. 1992).

Many European writers and theorists such as Eco, Grass, Wolf, and Müller have turned still more hopefully toward the past in order to negotiate the conflicts of the present. Frequently lacking Monk's cheerful enthusiasm for both past *and* present discourses, such Europeans tend to identify the postmodern condition with a far greater sense of calamity and stagnation than those more flexible multimedia artists and thinkers who most strikingly exemplify the positive parameters of the postmodern C-effect.

Note

1. Meredith Monk, interview with the author, 5 Feb. 1992. All subsequent references to this interview appear in the text.

99

Umberto Eco and the Re-turn to the
Middle Ages ❏

Like many B-effect theorists, the Italian semiotician and novelist Umberto Eco identifies the avant-garde tradition with the modernist era and suggests that both come to a standstill in the postmodern period. More specifically, Eco's *Reflections on "The Name of the Rose"* (1983) argues that the modernist/avant-garde impulse reaches a point where it produces "a metalanguage that speaks of impossible texts (conceptual art)" and therefore "can go no further."[1] It is certainly the case that the masterpieces of postmodern conceptual art, such as Piero Manzoni's signed lines, signed living sculptures and signed tins of *Artist's Shit* extend the definition of art so democratically and so dramatically that any further progress—or regress— seems impossible.[2] But it is equally evident that the same entropic conceptual impulse erupts within the modernist era, particularly in the notorious "silence of Marcel Duchamp."

Put very simply, both modernist *and* postmodernist artists sporadically assert that art can go no further. As one might also anticipate, one of postmodern culture's many strands consists of the systematic elaboration of Duchamp's conceptual aesthetic.

In this respect, Piero Manzoni, Ben Vautier, Joseph Kosuth, and other language and theory artists are very much what one might think of as "Junior Marcels," concerned more with the enunciation of conceptual paradoxes and impossibilities than any thing else.[3] Foucault's emphasis upon "the different concepts that enable us to conceive of discontinuity" and Derrida's wish "to transform concepts, to displace them, to turn them against their presuppositions, to reinscribe them in other chains, and little by little to modify the terrain of our work and thereby produce new configurations" suggest the way in which French poststructuralist theory similarly elaborates what Vautier terms "the Duchamp heritage."[4]

The obvious disadvantage of such approaches is that they frequently culminate in reductive retrospective intertextual or intercontextual dogma, asserting, for example, that "books are only made from other books and around other books," a conclusion that Eco partially shares and partially challenges. As he remarks, the writer who "plans something new" is not so much "a market analyst, cataloguing express demands" as "a philosopher who senses the patterns of the Zeitgeist" and who "wants to reveal to his public what it *should* want, even if it does not know it."[5]

Somewhat paradoxically, Eco asserts that postmodern thinkers may have to take one step backwards in order to take two steps forward, by "recognizing that the past . . . must be revisited." Stipulating that this recontemplation of the past must occur "with irony, not innocently," Eco's seemingly nostalgic claim that "the Middle Ages are the root of all our contemporary 'hot' problems" makes most sense as a reference to paradigmatic rather than causal parallels between the Middle Ages and the postmodern condition.[6] In Eco's terms, our era lends itself to definition "as a new Middle Ages" in the sense that it requires "new methods of adjustment" comparable to the "immense work of bricolage balanced among nostalgia, hope, and despair" that he perceives in the way in which the Middle Ages preserved the heritage of its past through "constant retranslation and reuse" (*Travels*, 65).

Repeatedly, Eco recommends "a culture of constant readjustment, fed on utopia" (*Travels*, 84) rather than acceptance of what he terms "the orphan syndrome of the disillusioned" (94). While Eco recognizes that "crisis sells well"—somewhat as Don DeLillo's novel *White Noise* (1984) subsequently satirizes the way that "only a catastrophe gets our attention"[7]—he wittily argues that indiscriminate use of this concept suggests "a case of editorial cramps" (*Travels*, 126). Equally perceptively, Eco suggests that a kind of generational, *theoretical* "cramps" seems to prevent the pillars of academia from emulating the effortless way in which the younger generation acknowledges and absorbs the positive creative potential of what he terms "a series of elements filtered through the mass media (and coming, in some cases, from the most impenetrable areas of our century's artistic expression)" (213–14).

Far more interesting than Eco's simplistic speculations regarding the hypothetical dead end of the avant-garde and the modern, these references to the continued impact and relevance of "our century's artistic experimentation" lead Eco to suggest, half seriously and half jokingly, that "all professors of theory of communications, trained by the texts of twenty years ago (this includes me) should be pensioned off" (*Travels*, 149).

Rather more critically pondering upon the way in which the Red Brigades represent the "last, incurable romantics" pledged to "upsetting the fine network of consensus, based on certain rules of living together" (*Travels*, 175), Eco concludes that

> the truth, actually, is less romantic. Certain modes of consensus are so essential to community life that they re-establish themselves despite every attempt to shake them. At most they are re-established in a more dogmatic, or should I say, more fanatic way. (177)

Offering muted enthusiasm for the "utopia of subversion" on the grounds that it only leads to the "reality of reaction" (*Travels*, 177), Eco's assessment of the postmodern condition seems most enlightening in terms of its proposition that the present era—like the Middle Ages—require responsible reconciliation of past, present, and evolving values and avoidance of academic conservativism, middle-class conservativism, and overly dogmatic modes of consensus.

On the one hand, Eco's cultural analyses lead him to ponder rather disappointedly upon the failure of flower power to produce anything other than a generation of yuppies reaffirming traditional middle-class values. Surveying patterns of rebellion and conservatism over the past three decades, Eco muses,

> In the homes of suburbia the average crew-cut executive still personifies the Roman of ancient virtues; but in the '60's and '70's his son let his hair grow in Indian style, wore a Mexican poncho, played his sitar, read Buddhist texts or Leninist pamphlets, and often succeeded (as in the late empire) in reconciling a dizzying variety of influences—such as Hesse, the zodiac, alchemy, the thoughts of Mao, marijuana, and urban guerrilla techniques. The generation of the '80's seems to be returning to the model of its fathers. But this phenomenon concerns

the upper middle class, not the kids we see break-dancing. (*Travels*, 76)

Eco's approving reference here to the energetic primitivism of the more or less urban "noble savages" that he sees break-dancing is complemented elsewhere by his manifest admiration for the younger generation's technological aptitudes and for what he terms the potential of "electronic dissent" against the "great systems" (*Travels*, 174). At their most inspiring, Eco's theories negotiate a position combining enthusiasm for both past and present, particularly the present that McLuhan associates with new mass media inaugurating "a new phase of history" and the capacity "to perceive the world in another way" (137).

Where Eco differs from McLuhan, he claims, is in his rejection of the new media's "call to narcotic passiveness" (*Travels*, 137) and in his insistence that "both medium and message" be conditioned by "the return to individual responsibility." Just as Cage and Chopin assert the necessity of dehexing the new media, Eco concludes, "To the anonymous divinity of Technological Communication our answer could be: 'Not Thy, but *our* will be done.' "(144).

Notes

1. Umberto Eco, *Reflections on "The Name of the Rose"*, trans. William Weaver (London: Secker and Warburg, 1983), 6.7.

2. See the catalog *Piero Manzoni: Paintings, Reliefs and Objects* (London: Tate Gallery, 1974).

3. For further discussions of Vautier and Kosuth, see *Artstudio*, no. 15 (Winter 1989).

4. Michel Foucault, *The Archeology of Knowledge and The Discourse on Language*, trans. A. M. Sheridan-Smith (New York: Pantheon, 1972), 5. Jacques Derrida, *Positions*, trans. Alan Bass (Chicago: Univ. of Chicago Press, 1981), 24. Ben Vautier, "The Duchamp Heritage," in *Dada Spectrum: The Dialectics of Revolt*, ed. Stephen Foster and Rudolf Kuenzli (Iowa: Coda and Univ. of Iowa Press, 1979), 249–258.

5. Eco, *Reflections*, 4.9.

6. Eco's comments about recontemplation of the past are found in Eco, *Reflections*, 6.7. His comments on the Middle Ages

as the root of contemporary problems appear in Eco, *Travels in Hyper-Reality*, trans. William Weaver (London: Picador, 1987), 65. All subsequent references to Eco's *Travels* appear in the text.

7. Don DeLillo, *White Noise* (London: Picador, 1986), 66. All subsequent references to this work appear in the text.

Grass and the Destruction of Mankind ❑

Like Umberto Eco, the German novelist Günter Grass detects certain parallels between the postmodern era and the Middle Ages in the sense that the present is "overtaken by . . . plagues, fear of demons, diffuse yearning for redemption, religious mania."[1]

Unlike Eco, Grass seems to have very little confidence in McLuhanesque notions of technological progress. As Grass indicates in *On Writing and Politics*, in his address "The Destruction of Mankind Has Begun" (1982), the very notion of the future strikes him as "questionable and in many respects unthinkable" given that "our present produces . . . poverty, hunger, polluted air, polluted bodies of water, forests destroyed by acid rain or deforestation, arsenals that seem to pile up of their own accord and are capable of destroying mankind many times over" (137). So far as Grass is concerned, humankind should be "capable of saying no to their inventions" and should be "prepared to forego the humanly possible and show some humility towards what's left of ruined nature" (140).

Reproaching postwar Europe both for its "ultra-rational" madness (*On Writing and Politics*, 74) and for "the new irrationality of technological mysticism" (116), Grass suggests that literature itself may have no future when faced with the task of defining "increasing modernization damage," and he pessimistically poses the question:

> Who will write about the slow death of Lake Constance? About the degradation and defence of the environment, the crisis in the educational system of a society dedicated to frenetic

achievement, about the surfeit that comes of glut? What writers will give these issues form and content while steering clear of the current jargon and ready-made formulas? (117)

Compounding his general critique of the mass media, Grass's article "What Shall We Tell Our Children?" (1979), also in *On Writing and Politics*, scathingly dismisses attempts at "mass enlightenment," such as television's "skindeep" *Holocaust* series, as "quite incapable of disclosing the complex 'modernity' of genocide and the many-layered responsibilities at the root of it" (88).

Elsewhere, Grass predicts that increasingly sophisticated modes of mass surveillance will completely usurp private space:

Inveterate perfectionism, unlimited faith in technological progress, the government's excessive zeal in combating terrorism and a well-nigh hysterical security-mindedness have opened the way to . . . data banks, listening devices, electronic identity cards—in short, the transparent society. (*On Writing and Politics*, 143–44)

Such technologies, Grass surmises, "not only foreshadow a police state" but already provide "an advance sampling of its practice" (144).

Despite his specific political commitment to the S.P.D., Grass's more general comments place very little confidence in his immediate contemporaries. Passing final judgment upon the two main middle-aged characters in his novel *Headbirths or The Germans Are Dying Out* (1980), Grass's evaluation is short but sour: "Seldom has a generation exhausted itself so quickly; *either* they crack up or they stop taking risks."[2]

Like Eco, Grass finally places particular confidence in "the younger generation that is willing to take risks" (*Headbirths*, 148). Offering this prospect a rather trite fictional formulation in *Headbirths*, the last page of this novel describes its central couple sitting dumbstruck in their "well preserved VW," "not knowing what to say in German," as "more and more children, all foreign . . . all cheerful," materialize around them "from side streets and backyards, from all directions" (128).

Notes

1. Günter Grass, *On Writing and Politics*, trans. Ralph Manheim (Harmondsworth, Eng.: Penguin, 1987), 73. All subsequent references to this work appear in the text.
2. Günter Grass, *Headbirths or The Germans Are Dying Out*, trans. Ralph Manheim (Harmondsworth, Eng.: Penguin, 1984), 127. All subsequent references to this novel appear in the text.

Grass, Mann, and the Re-turn to Forbidden Literature ❏

As Grass points out in his conversations with the novelist Salman Rushdie, his fiction deliberately contrives to evoke recent German history by recourse to "the German Romantic tradition" and "all this forbidden literature, the early expressionism in German, the surrealistic authors."[1] Explaining how this leads to a fiction in which "in one sentence I jump from flat reality that you see . . . to inside things" ("Fictions Are Lies," 14), Grass argues that the use of fairy tales reveals "a much much, richer truth" than flat realism. In other words, "We have many realities. Our problem is that we don't accept that there are many realities. This side wants only this reality, and the other only their reality. This is one of the reasons why we still have this struggle" (15).

It seems strange that Grass should still have felt compelled to struggle for the right to mix different kinds of fictional reality in the mid-eighties, some quarter century after he had first integrated these techniques in *The Tin Drum* (1958). Grass's allusions to forbidden discourses of expressionism and surrealism doubtless echo general memories of their stigmatization as degenerate in the Hitler era—an era when, as Grass observes in an autobiographical section of *Headbirths*, "National Socialist ideology robbed the German language of its meaning, had corrupted it and laid waste whole fields of words" (12). Accordingly, as Grass explains,

106

In this mutilated language, writers, handicapped by its injuries began to stammer more than write. Their helplessness was measured against Thomas Mann and Brecht, the giants of refugee literature; measured against their already classical greatness, only stammering could assert itself. (*Headbirths*, 12)

Strongly reminiscent of Beckett's claim that he too could only work with "impotence, ignorance," whereas Joyce "was making words do the absolute maximum of work," Grass's feelings of inferiority towards Mann and Brecht typify the difficulty that many European postmodern novelists appear to experience in breaking free from what Baudrillard might term "the abominable weight" of Modernist culture.[2]

As these pages have indicated, European avant-garde techno-poets and eco-poets—such as Henri Chopin and Joseph Beuys—confidently distinguish themselves from the Blériots and Duchamps of modernism, while the American multimedia artist Robert Wilson has been acclaimed by the veteran surrealist Aragon for creating "what we others, who fathered surrealism . . . dreamed it might become."[3] By contrast, a number of European postmodern novelists tend either to belittle themselves by comparison with modernism's fictional masters or to derive somewhat nostalgic—and somewhat familiar—impetus from the innovations of modernism's verbal-visual avant-gardes.

Robbe-Grillet, for example, elaborates what one might think of as an inexpressive cubist fiction, which—in his own terms—transmutes into a slightly more original partially cubist, partially surrealist cinema, such as *L'année dernière à Marienbad* (1961). Grass, by contrast, like the Italian and German artists that Bonito-Oliva associates with the antitechnological, neo-expressionist *trans-avant-garde*, creates a volatile, predominantly expressionistic poetic.

In Grass's terms, his writing stammers when compared with Mann's majestic prose. Considered in the terms of Bonito-Oliva's *Trans-avantgarde International*, Grass's narratives might more flatteringly be said to "[let] the image ride without asking where it comes from or where it is going, following drifts of pleasure which also re-establish the primacy of the intensity of the work over that of the technique" (66). While both Grass's novels and trans-avant-garde painting prioritize intensity rather than technique, Grass's practice differs quite significantly from Bonito-Oliva's hedonistic aesthetic in terms of its highly serious, satirical intent.

As Grass's characters in *Headbirths* often remark, the images in his fiction seem alive with alarming connotations. A bat, for example, appears to be "an incarnation of all the horrors facing them in the eighties" (76). By contrast, Bonito-Oliva associates the neo-expressionist painting of the trans-avant-garde with "uninhibited superficiality" and argues that its mythological references simply serve as occasions for images "relieved of any weight that [they] may have borne" (68).

At this point, it seems evident that Grass's dilemma, like Beuys's dilemma, is the problem of identifying a mythology capable of translating contemporary concerns with sufficient impact and integrity to justify both retreat from postmodern technology and from "classical" modernist models and recourse to the more ancient realm of archetypal figures. Once again, the most interesting modes of postmodern creativity evince the positive impulse that Hassan associates with "provisional reconstructions" and "pragmatic remythifications"[4] and that Eco identifies as processes of "readjustment . . . retranslation and reuse" (*Travels*, 84).

That Grass cautiously considers his writings to be mere stammering is at best a generous gesture of respect to his modernist masters or at worst, a gesture of uncertainty on Grass's part. More urgent, perhaps, is the question of whether Grass's literary mythology lapses into superficial nostalgia or whether it functions more contemporaneously as a bridge between the languages and the assumptions of past and present.

Beuys, for example, insisted that he did not literally want "to go back to the magical or mythical world" but desired to pursue a visual analysis of the present by allusion to these domains.[5] In Beuys's terms, "This is not regression; the only question at hand is progression and by what method one can further progression" (qtd. in *Beuys: Life and Works*, 72).

Uncomfortably caught between a compulsion to satirize the present, without the consolation of any particular hope in the future, or of entire confidence in his premodernist mythology and his stammering multileveled, postclassical discourse, Grass typifies the disquietude of those Europeans lacking the utopian confidence of Eco, Chopin, and Beuys.

Notes

1. Günter Grass and Salman Rushdie, "Fictions Are Lies that Tell the Truth," a conversation, *The Listener*, 27 June 1985, 15. All subsequent references to this conversation appear in the text.
2. Samuel Beckett, qtd. in "Moody Man of Letters," sec. 2, 3. Baudrillard, *America*, 93.
3. Louis Aragon, "Open Letter to André Breton, 2nd June 1971," trans. Linda Moses, Jean-Paul Lavergne, and George Ashley, in the program for *Hamletmachine*, London, Almeida Theatre, 1987, unpaginated.
4. Hassan, *The Postmodern Turn*, 204.
5. Joseph Beuys, qtd. by Gotz Adriani, Winfried Konnertz, and Karin Thomas in *Joseph Beuys: Life and Works*, trans. Patricia Lech (New York: Barron's Educational Services, 1979), 71. All subsequent references to this work appear in the text.

Ernst, Carrington, and the Re-turn of Surrealism ❏

Writing on women artists and the surrealist movement, Whitney Chadwick quotes Dorothea Tanning's observation that "the place of woman in Surrealism was no different than her place in bourgeois society in general" and Jacqueline Lamba's suggestion that "women were still undervalued. It was very hard to be a woman painter."[1] As the partners of Max Ernst and André Breton, Tanning and Lamba presumably knew the surrealist movement as well as anybody else and had good reasons to criticize it in this way. Chadwick in turn points out that almost without exception, women artists viewed themselves as having functioned independently of Breton's inner circle and the shaping of Surrealist doctrine. Many of them were younger than their male colleagues; most of them were just embarking on their lives as artists when they first encountered Surrealism and would do their mature work after leaving the group. Their involvement was defined by personal relationships, networks of friends and lovers, not by active participation in an inner circle dominated by Breton's presence. (*Women Artists*, 11)

Considered in this way, surrealism seems to lend itself to redefinition in terms of two distinct phases: a *B-phase*, dominated by Breton's presence and by the work of male artists such as Ernst, Dali, and Tanguy, and a *C-phase*, composed of artists such as Ernst's sometime partner Leonora Carrington, Jacqueline Lamba Breton, Kay Sage Tanguy, Dorothea Tanning Ernst, and Remidios Varo Peret.

As Chadwick indicates, the British painter and writer Leonora Carrington typifies the independence of the C-phase surrealist. Reconsidering Breton's proposal that the male artist should "make visible everything that is part of the feminine, as opposed to the masculine, system of the world" and "appropriate to himself everything that distinguishes woman from man,"[2] Carrington bluntly responded "bullshit" (Chadwick, *Women Artists,* 66). In a text written in 1976 for a retrospective exhibition in New York, Carrington herself proposes an alternative, predominantly mythological and feminist surrealist agenda, predicated upon "the mysteries which were ours." She wittily concludes,

> Most of us, I hope, are now aware that a woman should not have to demand Rights. The Rights were there from the beginning; they must be Taken Back Again, including the mysteries which were ours and which were violated, stolen or destroyed, leaving us with the thankless hope of pleasing a male animal, probably of one's own species. (Chadwick, *Women Artists,* 218)

Carrington's novel *The Hearing Trumpet* (1974) similarly rejects the "demonological sacrilegious religion" of "the Angry Father God" in favor of a "magic law" associated with the Holy

Grail, "the Great Mother" and such mysterious creatures as "Anubeth . . . a wolf-headed woman . . . finely proportioned, and, apart from the head, entirely human."[3]

On first reading, such descriptions clearly coincide with Max Ernst's suggestion in "What Is the Mechanism of Collage?" (1936), that the surreal image should represent *the coupling of two realities; irreconcilable in appearance, upon a plane which apparently does not suit them.*[4] Significantly though, Carrington's coupling of wolf and woman is not so much a hallucinatory fusion of images "upon a plane that does not suit them" as an evocation of a utopian creature on a plane that *does* suit her. The narrator comments: "It would be a great pity if werewolves died out altogether. . . . After all animal-headed Goddesses and Gods have inspired us all through history" (*Hearing Trumpet*, 154).

Carrington's Anubeth is at once both an idealized mythological figure, literally embodying animal and human values, and a very contemporary werewolf, whose aristocratic uncle suffered "during the Communist persecution of Hungary," "especially as he came from such a noble family" (*Hearing Trumpet*, 153). Considered in these contexts, Carrington's C-phase surrealism seems most significant as a poetic model for pragmatic cerebral, psychic, social, and environmental change.

Similarly utopian aspirations clearly motivated Beuys to demonstrate his solidarity with animals in such actions as *Coyote* (1974) and *How to Explain Paintings to a Dead Hare* (1965) and similar perceptions prompt Grass's observation: "We are not alone here. There are animals, there is nature. We have to find another connection to nature . . . we have to go on to tell stories."[5]

Notes

1. Whitney Chadwick, *Women Artists and the Surrealist Movement* (London: Thames and Hudson, 1985), 11. All subsequent references to this work appear in the text. See also, *Leonora Carrington: Paintings, Drawings and Sculptures 1940–1990*, ed. Andrea Schlieker (London: Serpentine Gallery, 1991).

2. Breton, "What Is Surrealism?" 65.

3. Leonora Carrington, *The Hearing Trumpet* (San Francisco: City Lights, 1976), 146, 151. All subsequent references to this work appear in the text.

4. Max Ernst, "What is the Mechanism of Collage?" (1936), trans. Dorothea Tanning, in *Theories of Modern Art*, 427.

5. Günter Grass and Salman Rushdie, "Writing for a Future," in *Voices: Writers and Politics*, ed. Bill Bourne (Nottingham, Eng.: Spokesman, 1987), 56.

Carrington, Cage, Beuys, and the Poetics of Resistance ❑

While Carrington and Grass redefine and redeploy folkloric and surreal stories in response to aspects of contemporary social, sexual, and environmental politics, Beuys's individual and collective actions transport this sensibility still more directly into the public arena, with both predictable and unpredictable results. On the one hand, as the following exchange between Beuys and Willoughby Sharp indicates, Beuys's claims simply strike the average onlooker as "crazy":

Beuys: Two years ago I created a political party for animals.
Sharp: Do you have a lot of animals in the party?
Beuys: It's the largest party in the world.
Sharp: And you are the leader?
Beuys: I am the leader.
Sharp: You're crazy. (*Laughter*)
Beuys: And therefore I am a very mighty man. Mightier
          than Nixon. (*More laughter*)
                              (Beuys, "Interview with Sharp," 81)

Clearly, Sharp considers Beuys's project to be excessively poetic, to put it mildly. On the other hand, as Cage pointed out in a late interview with Francesco Bonami, Beuys's poetic, pedagogic, and political initiatives—such as his International Free University—also appear distinctly pragmatic. Beuys was, after all, a cofounder of the Green Party, as well as the Animal

Party. As Cage indicates in his comments below, Beuys's thought suggests two modes of utopian optimism: the individual and the institutional.

He differed from me insofar as he tended towards defined organization. I think the International Free University was a really interesting project, as was all his work. He always had very good ideas, his point of view involved the whole of humanity. I agree with his optimism and utopia. Unfortunately, I realize that humanity is increasingly at an impasse which makes my ideal society more and more improbable.[1]

Carrington's utopian vision of a postchauvinist ideal society, motivated by what she defines as "microscopic knowledge of the earth, its plants and creatures" (qtd. in Chadwick, 199), is significant precisely as a transitional point between Breton's early surrealist aspiration to identify absolute reality, "certain that I shall never share in it," and the rather different modes of postmodern pragmatic/poetic feminist surrealism and pragmatic/poetic eco-political surrealism, asserting mysteries, rights, and values that "were there from the beginning."[2]

Cage's and Beuys's creative projects clearly share similar motivations. While Cage conceded that his utopian hopes for broadly based social change seem increasingly improbable, he still advocated the same kind of *personal* poetics of resistance that Beuys in turn associated with "the strongest of spirits, who are able to resist in the middle of the shit . . . and who feel that their own ability can only grow in the middle of problems."[3]

Asked by Bonami how one might overcome the present "impasse," Cage stirringly replied, "Answer the telephone! I mean, keep in contact, don't isolate yourself. If humanity doesn't force itself to keep its lines of communication open, I'm afraid we'll never manage to live in a better world."[4] Like Carrington, Cage and Beuys argue for a practical surreal project in the sense that they consistently combine what Cage terms "elements paradoxical by nature" within the kind of aesthetically and politically relevant projects that Beuys envisaged as "bridging between extremities" and as encouraging subsequent "social organisms . . . constructed after this idea."[5]

Notes

1. John Cage, interview with Francesco Bonami, *Flash Art* (international ed.) 24.160 (October 1991): 95.
2. Breton, "What Is Surrealism?" 414.
3. Joseph Beuys, "Interview with Wijers, 254.
4. Cage, *Flash Art*, 95.
5. Cage, "Defence of Satie," 84. Beuys, "Plight," 8.

Cage, Carrington, Barthes, Burroughs, Bense: From Artha *to* Moksha ❏

Discussing the function of chance operations in his work and remarking that "a lot of people think I should use chance operations in everything I do," Cage suggests that the "typically Western concept" of consistent, invariable thought might be replaced by Indian philosophy's "four different ways of using the mind."

> The first is called *Artha*, your instincts for survival, which is what keeps you from getting hit by a car when you cross the street. The second is *Karma*, pleasure. The third, *Dharma*, which belongs to rituals and religion. The last is *Moksha*, the fourth and final mind state which frees us from the other three. Only when the mind reaches *Moksha* can you achieve chance operations.[1]

The impulses of the C-effect make particular sense when viewed within this kind of context. Without necessarily sharing the four Indian concepts to which Cage alludes, postmodern artists consistently evoke new forms of art in terms of a *third* concept, beyond conventional binary oppositions.

Carrington, for example, discusses her quest for female spirituality as an attempt to become the *third person* "of the Trinity" (qtd. in Chadwick, *Women Artists,* 199). Barthes rather similarly challenges structuralist rhetoric when he posits the existence of *third meanings*, existing "outside (articulated) language," where "another language begins" in such a way that

114

"a semantologist would not agree to its objective existence."[2] William Burroughs and Brion Gysin refer in turn to the concept of the *third mind*—a "third, invisible, intangible force" and "unseen collaborator," which is "there when two minds collaborate."[3] Bense rather more literally refers to the *three-dimensional* quality of concrete poetry in the sense that it simultaneously orchestrates language in three dimensions, verbally, vocally, and visually, irrespective of the usual requirements of the "possible sentence."[4]

Whether metaphorical or literal, such third and three-dimensional concepts seem most significant in terms of their assertion of *synthetic* possibilities beyond dialectical thought, work, and composition. To some extent, the same impulse motivates Jameson's notion of a collective *third possibility* "beyond the old bourgeois self" as well as the East German writer Christa Wolf, who emphasizes what she terms the "smiling vital force" of a *third alternative* beyond the "clear-cut distinctions" of "one-sided male rationalism," and her compatriot, Heiner Müller, who advocates the existential energy of the *third world* (*Germania*, 33) as an antidote to the "schizophrenic position" of his own existence on each side (32) of Eastern and Western Europe.[5]

Notes

1. Cage, *Flash Art*, 93.
2. Barthes, "The Third Meaning," 61, 65.
3. William S. Burroughs and Brion Gysin, *The Third Mind* (London: John Calder, 1979), 25, 19.
4. Max Bense, "Concrete Poetry," 74.
5. Jameson, *Flash Art*, 70. Christa Wolf, *Cassandra: A Novel and Four Essays* (1983), trans. Jan van Heurck (London: Virago, 1985), 106, 244. All subsequent references to this work appear in the text.

Cage, Wolf, and the Re-turn to
the Third Alternative ☐

In many respects both the problems outlined by Günter Grass—and the solutions outlined by Carrington and Cage—find their double in the writings of the East German novelist Christa Wolf. Recently accused of withholding sufficiently forthright comment on East German culture, Wolf can perhaps best be understood in terms of the reasons that persuaded her that the most relevant way to "set such a thing as 'the living word' against the contemporary necrophilia, which manifests itself in steel, glass and concrete" is to use language that "would be inconspicuous and seek to name the inconspicuous, the precious everyday, the concrete" (*Cassandra*, 270).

As these and other arguments in Wolf's four essays in *Cassandra: A Novel and Four Essays* (1983) suggest, Wolf's meditations upon contemporary society and upon the prefiguration of the present social, political, and cultural problems that she perceived in the *Cassandra* legend led her to celebrate such everyday pleasures as the view of a particular cherry tree in a meadow—"I do not know of another one like it"—glimpsed in a "soft serene light, indescribable"—while planting "the last flower seeds for the year" to the accompanying "noise of passing armoured tanks" (255). Embodying similar ecological and ritualistic concerns, Anchises, a benign sage in *Cassandra*, "never had a tree chopped down without first conferring with it at length; without first removing from it a seed or a twig which he could plant in the earth to ensure its continued existence" (92).

It is perhaps with reference to Anchises's preoccupation with the inconspicuous ritual of continued existence—and one might add of *coexistence* and the conviction that one should "talk with everyone" and "shouldn't give up on anyone until he's dead" (93)—that Wolf suggests in her *Four Essays* that *Cassandra* functions not so much as a nostalgic "description of bygone days" as "a model for a kind of utopia" (224).

Wolf's specification in her essays that her novel only evokes

116

"a kind of utopia" rather than an unambiguously definitive utopian blueprint stems from her reluctance to contribute to "the dead end into which sectarian thinking . . . invariably leads" (*Cassandra*, 260). Exemplifying the dangers of "seeing what we want to see" (201), in terms of feminist readings of Minoan culture, Wolf's essays point out how strategic neglect of the ways in which "the Minoans used slave labor, male and of course, female, too" (202) facilitated the process by which

> Crete was . . . turned into the Promised Land of those who looked to the past to satisfy their longings—namely feminists . . . who, hard-pressed as they were by the experience of the present and fears about the future, saw in the Minoan kingdoms the social bodies to which they could concretely match their utopian speculations and yearnings. (200)

Caught between the twin perils of alternating modes of sectarianism—local, political dogmatism or atemporal, mythological dogmatism, "masculinity mania," and "femininity mania" (*Cassandra*, 260)—Wolf attempts to negotiate a more modest position, looking for "alternatives . . . other than 'Red' and 'dead' " (252).

Becoming increasingly aware of "other realities . . . which our five agreed-upon senses do not grasp: for which reason we must deny them," Wolf's fictional Cassandra gradually envisages what she terms a *third alternative* to the binary mentality. On the one hand, she offers the following critique of Greek logic:

> For the Greeks there is no alternative but either truth or lies, right or wrong, victory or defeat, friend or enemy, life or death. They think differently than we do. What cannot be seen, smelled, heard, touched, does not exist. It is the other alternative that they crush between their clear-cut distinctions, the third alternative, which in their view, does not exist, the smiling vital force that is able to generate itself from itself over and over: the undivided, spirit in life, life in spirit. (*Cassandra*, 106–7)

On the other hand, Wolf's characters posit that "between killing and dying there is a third alternative: living" (118), confirming Cassandra's sense that they can only endure if they "can stop being victorious" (116). Not surprisingly, Wolf's essays approvingly quote Heiner Müller's maxim—from his play *Quartett*—that "it is good to be a woman and no victor" (*Cassandra*, 296).

Wolf, Mann, and the Authority of Literary Genres ❑

Wolf's overall dilemma is that, unlike Müller, she finds it difficult to identify an adequate literary form for her concerns. Somewhat as her character Cassandra comments, "Nothing left to describe the world but the language of the past" (*Cassandra*, 14), Wolf's essays insist upon the "unsayable" (226) quality of the postmodern condition; upon the way in which her "awareness of the incongruousness of words keeps growing" (226); and more generally, upon her generation's "tiredness of hope" and its growing sense that "indignation, revolt would be inappropriate" (236).

Wolf's essays indicate that she can no longer "accept the authority of the literary genres" (*Cassandra*, 278), yet at the same time she remains uncertain how to define an alternative poetics. While she approvingly quotes Lewis Mumford's *Myth of the Machine* as a model for an alternative *ethic* asserting "inner change" and the restoration of "autonomy and initiative to the . . . individual soul" (265), Wolf argues that an "aesthetic of *resistance* to it all has yet to be developed" (236).

It is as this point, that Wolf's essays refer to two quite different facets of modernism: the dichotomy that one might perhaps define as the "Woolf-Mann effect." On the one hand, Wolf aligns herself with her English namesake, suggesting that she "no longer wants to create large scale, vital, ideal figures" within "coherent stories" but would rather employ the kind of "narrative network" that the prose of Virginia Woolf seems to "require and endorse" as an alternative to "linear narrative" (*Cassandra*, 262). Rather than attempting to employ "the strictly one-track-minded approach—the extraction of a single 'skein' for purposes of narration and study," Wolf proposes to evoke the "entire fabric" in terms of "the feeling that everything is fundamentally related" (287).

This decision leads in turn to her critique of the overshadowing presence of what Grass would term the "classical" modernism of Thomas Mann. Consideration of Mann's assertions in a letter to Karl Kerenyi (1934) that he is "no friend of the anti-intellectual movement" (which he specifically associates here with supporters of the National Socialist Party) and that "the present day . . . rancour against the development of the human cerebrum . . . has always struck me as a snobbish and ridiculous form of self-negation" (qtd. in *Cassandra*, 243) leads Wolf to the more general, slightly ahistorical supposition that modernists like Mann seem to have confused positive modes of extrarationality with negative modes of antirationality. "Worth pondering even today: how the criticism of one-sided male rationalism runs the risk of being wrongly interpreted as irrationalism, hostility to science, and also put to wrong use" (244).

Wolf's deliberations upon the right and wrong uses of different kinds of rational and extrarational critique—and upon what she sees here as the counterproductive workings of Mann's "intellectual conscience"—culminate in her diagnosis of the seemingly endemic self-doubt that she discerns both in the late modernist years, as "spreading darkness eclipsed almost all Europe climaxing in World War II," and in her own time, in "the acrid disappointment of the postwar years" (*Cassandra*, 241).

Ironically, for all its reservations regarding the validity and advisability of such self-doubt, Wolf's own writing frequently erupts in expressions of fatalistic bafflement. Noting that "an uneasiness which many file under the names of emptiness and loss of meaning makes most people afraid," Wolf's essays finally sum up her sense of the European social and political situation in the following assertion of profound disbelief regarding the possibility of either local or more distant "new directions": "We cannot hope that the used-up institutions, to which many were accustomed will supply a new direction. Run a zig-zag course.

But there is no escape route in sight. . . . Australia is not a way out (*Cassandra*, 239).

Focusing still more specifically upon the erstwhile reality of the Berlin Wall, a diary entry for 30 December 1980 records Wolf's still more fatalistic convictions that "changes within the two German states are unthinkable," that "there is no scope for change" and "there is no revolutionary situation," affirmations that she then rather tentatively counters with the question, "Or is that not how things are at all?" (*Cassandra*, 237–38).

Discussing the same possibility in an interview of 1988, Wolf's fellow East Berliner, writer Heiner Müller, firmly insisted: "It won't disappear in my lifetime. That's out of the question" (*Germania*, 65). Like Wolf's writings and statements, Müller's responses to the postmodern condition typify the European intellectual's vulnerability to the general mythologies of the B-effect and to what Grass's *Headbirths* designates "modernization damage" (13).

Müller, Beuys, and the Elevation of the Berlin Wall ❑

Heiner Müller's position in the European postmodern cosmos is best introduced by reference to Joseph Beuys's suggestion that "the idealistic poets and philosophers such as Wolfgang von Goethe, Novalis and others who saw Germany as being in this middle position, bridging between extremities," all prefigure the ways in which contemporary German culture should still aspire above all to "bridging" and "helping others."[1]

For Beuys, "the function of the German" is that of living "in the middle of Europe," of belonging to "the middle European countries," and therefore of "being a mediator and finding the bridge position in the centre of Europe." Predictably, Beuys concluded that Germany in the mid-eighties seemed "exactly the opposite to a bridge": "There is the Berlin Wall so there is no possibility to mediate between extremities which are always coming from the east and from the west."[2]

Somewhat as Joshua modified Jericho's walls with instrumental impact, Beuys attempted to neutralize the spiritual barriers brought about by the Berlin Wall by responding with the ironical proposal that it be transformed by slight alteration into the equivalent of a Duchampian ready-made. More specifically, Beuys's C.V. for 1964 includes the detail: "Beuys recommends that the Berlin Wall be elevated by 5 cm (better proportions!)" (qtd. in *Beuys: Life and Works*, 105).

Writing in some detail to the North Rhine-Westphalia Department of the Interior, in order to clarify the symbolic function of this proposal, Beuys explains that far from constituting literal endorsement of the wall, his plea for improved proportions functions primarily to indicate the way in which what he rather ambiguously terms "realistic spiritual training" might liberate the young from the kind of entrenched fatalism that Christa Wolf's essays associate with "the older, clarified members" of her generation (*Cassandra*, 238). Beuys recommends:

> The contemplation of the Berlin Wall from an optical angle that takes into account only the proportions of this construction should still be allowed. Disarm the Wall immediately. Through inner laughter.
>
> Annihilate the Wall. Do not keep hanging on any more to the physical Wall. To be directed to the spiritual Wall and to conquer this, that is what it is all about. . . .
>
> Spontaneously generated question: What part of my character or of that of other men has let this thing come into being? How much of each one of us contributed to this Wall being possible and continues to contribute to it? Is everyone sufficiently interested in the disappearance of this Wall? What antiegotistical, antimaterialistic, what sort of realistic spiritual schooling are young people receiving to conquer this?
>
> Quintessence: The Wall as such is totally unimportant. Don't talk so much about the Wall! Establish through self-education a better morale in mankind and all walls will disappear. There are so many small walls between you and me. (qtd. in *Beuys: Life and Works*, 114, 116)

While Heiner Müller has much to say about the material and spiritual walls separating individuals and nations, his own appraisal of the Berlin Wall seems the very reverse of Beuys's recommendations. Discussing the potential reunification of Berlin in an interview with Sylvère Lotringer, Müller rather surprisingly confides:

> Frankly, I wouldn't like that to happen for the next ten years. . . . I believe in conflict. I don't believe in anything else. What I try to do in my writings is to strengthen the sense of conflicts, to strengthen confrontations and contradictions. There is no other way. I'm not interested in answers and solutions. I don't have any to offer. I'm interested in problems and conflicts. (*Germania*, 34)

In a sense, both Beuys and Müller are poets of conflict. But whereas actions such as in Beuys's *Coyote: I Like America and America Likes Me* simultaneously dramatize conflict (the persecution of the coyote and the American Indian) and resolution (Beuys's symbolic coexistence with the coyote, with the American Indian, and with America), Müller's poetic barbs tend to accentuate and aggravate points of conflict and contradiction.

Elsewhere in his interview with Lotringer, Müller nonchalantly observes, "What I like about the Berlin Wall is that it is a sign for a real situation, the situation the world is in. And here you have it in concrete. One can see the end of history more clearly from here" (*Germania*, 37).

By "the end of history," Müller appears to imply several things: the accumulative consequences of past history, the likely momentum of present historical trends, and his more general conviction that "there is no more history in Western Europe," that "the European concept of history is over," and that "there can't be any progress in the West" (*Germania*, 16). As the events of late 1989 demonstrated, Müller's predictions were not entirely accurate.

Notes

1. Beuys, "Plight," 8.
2. Beuys, "Plight," 8.

Müller, Brecht, and the Petrification
of Hope ☐

As a writer capable of traveling in the two Germanies, and
from East Germany to America, Müller finds himself in unusual
circumstances. On the one hand he savors his "schizophrenic
position" between East and West conceding, "I like to stand
with one leg on each side of the wall" (*Germania*, 32–33). On
the other hand, Müller anticipates considerable consolation
from the prospect of witnessing the eventual eclipse of Western
culture by "the Third World . . . the great threat for the West
and the great hope for our side" (33). Somewhat as Eco romanti-
cizes the primitive vitality of urban break-dancers (*Travels*,
76), Müller provocatively designates illiterates as "the hope for
literature" (*Germania*, 118) and equates "the murals of the
minorities and the proletarian subway art, created with stolen
paints by anonymous hands," with "*the realm of freedom*, which
lies beyond privilege" (117).

In this respect, Müller's vision hovers between born-again
surrealism, born-again romantic folklorism, born-again Eco-
medievalism, and born-again Brechtian modernism. As Müller
indicates in an interview of 1981 with Harun Farocki, his admiration for Brecht's writings stems from his sense that they are
"much more medieval, much more bound to the provincial in
the positive sense of the term" than neo-Brechtians, such as
the French filmmaker Jean-Luc Godard, might assume. Müller
further explains,

> I mean for the foreigner Brecht is a very different figure than
> for us. If you know Brecht from translations, you get a com-
> pletely different picture, because the regional is lost, and the
> pre-Renaissance qualities in Brecht, as well as the agrarian.
> Godard probably perceived Brecht as an industrial author, not
> as a poet of the peasants. (*Germania*, 164)

Elsewhere, Müller systematically dissociates himself from
both Brecht's poetics and discursive framework. Discussing
Hamletmachine with Carl Weber, for example, Müller suggests
that while Brecht evokes "a description of people missing the

occasions and chances of history," his own work is not so much about the processes of catastrophe as about a postcatastrophic era. "It is about the results of missed occasions, about history as a story of chances lost. That is more than plain disappointment, it is description of the petrification of hope, and consequently an effort to formulate a despair to distance myself from it."[1]

Müller's emphasis upon cathartic despair, as opposed to more Brechtian dialectical analysis, clearly stems from his sense that "the net of Brecht's dramaturgy was too wide-meshed for the microstructure of new problems" (Germania, 130) and his concomitant conviction that "a story which has 'hands and feet,' the fable in its classical definition," can no longer "grasp today's reality any more."[2]

Not surprisingly, many of Müller's protagonists, such as the "actor playing Hamlet" in Hamletmachine, deny their own dramatic identity and authenticity in outbursts such as, "I'm not Hamlet. I don't take part any more. My words have nothing to tell any more. . . . My drama doesn't happen any more."[3] Like his Hamlet figure, Müller is best defined as what he calls—in the following Brechtian formula—"the man between the ages who knows that the old age is obsolete" yet who also finds that "the new age has barbarian features he simply cannot stomach."[4] Put another way, Müller seems to be trapped behind a *time wall* preventing him from ever sharing the same "track" as Western European and American culture.

Introduced in terms of an apocryphal reference to the way in which this kind of conceptual barrier prevented the German Wehrmacht from "entering Moscow during the Second World War"—"they just stood there. They couldn't go further" (Germania, 13)—Müller's concept of the time wall offers the perfect image for the equally strange conceptual forces, which apparently dissuade Müller from making some sort of bridge between the different sites of postmodern culture.

At best Müller maintains an ambiguous love-hate relationship with the "New World" of America, warming to it as "the most innocent nation in the Western world" and yet deploring its naivety as a culture "that didn't experience the Holocaust."[5]

This relationship culminates in several English language editions of Müller's writings; in considerable critical attention; and in his remarkable association with the multimedia artist and director Robert Wilson in the collaborations that Müller likens to "two friendly machines, communicating with mutual regard for each other" (*Germania*, 80).

Notes

1. Heiner Müller, qtd. in "The Despair and the Hope," by Carl Weber, *Performing Arts Journal* 4.3 (1980): 138.
2. Müller, qtd. in "The Despair and the Hope," 139.
3. Heiner Müller, *Hamletmachine*, trans. Carl Weber, *Performing Arts Journal* 4.3 (1980): 144.
4. Müller, qtd. in "The Despair and the Hope," 137.
5. Müller, qtd. in "A Conversation with Robert Wilson and Heiner Müller," by Arthur Holmberg, *Modern Drama* 31.3 (Sept. 1988): 458.

Müller, Wilson, and the Re-turn to the Classics ❏

The compatibility between Müller's and Wilson's "machines" is that of inquisitive antitheses. In Müller's terms, Wilson's machine "works differently and I want to use it" (*Germania*, 80). Despite his avowed attraction to conflict, Müller's collaborative work with Wilson offers yet another instance of the reconciliatory momentum of late postmodern creativity or at least, of the creative *tensions* within late postmodern theater.

Wilson, for his part, comments that what he likes best in Müller's work is "the humour in his writings, as well as the density of his texts": "On the surface, Heiner's texts appear to be very compressed, dark, and at times, political and even violent. But with further investigation, one sees there is an underlying humour which makes the play strong, terrifying."[1]

Müller, by contrast, suggests that Wilson's work is perhaps most interesting for its lightness and its absence of political precision, qualities that lead Müller, like so many before him, to refer once again to the New World noble savage: "What interests me in Bob Wilson is precisely that he doesn't know politics in his mind. He's an American Indian in a way, an Indian from Texas. . . . History for him includes animals, clouds, space. That's what I like in him, these Indian roots" (*Germania*, 78–79).

Both Wilson and Müller are drawn together by their parallel explorations of multifaceted textual fragmentation. Wilson, for example, expresses his enthusiasm for the freedom that Müller's texts offer the director.

> The density of his texts derives from their volume of contradictions, which makes interpretation impossible. There is no one way to read them . . . one frequently does not know who is to say what line, or where the text is to be placed in terms of setting. . . . Ultimately, what one is left with are a lot of questions. (interview with author, 5 Feb. 1991)

In turn, it is precisely Wilson's capacity to work with "a lot of questions" without attempting to rationalize their implications into a single coherent message that seems to make him the ideal collaborator from Müller's point of view. Insisting that his work can "speak for itself" and complaining that most German directors "don't respect the text as a reality in itself," Müller notes with some satisfaction that "Wilson never interprets."

> He just gets the text and tries to find room for it. . . . I think a good text has to be like a thing, like a solid rock or stone. . . . Robert Wilson just takes it like a kid playing with marbles. He just watches the marbles. But . . . here in Germany they always try to find something inside.[2]

All of this is not to suggest either that Wilson works randomly with Müller's texts or that Müller's texts work randomly with language and contain nothing *inside*. Rather, it would appear that against all odds, Müller's post-Brechtian drama and Wilson's post-Cageian production techniques quite unexpectedly bridge the time walls separating East German and Lower East Side theatrical experiment.

While Müller's evocations of social, political, and historical crises tend to be more culturally specific than Wilson's more symbolic and metaphysical images, both Müller and Wilson insist that audiences must read between the lines of their respective materials. Distinguishing East German audiences from their Western counterparts, Müller comments, "They can easily recognize, or see or feel the silence between words, between sentences. They know what is going on between the words. They bring in their own experience. People in the West don't. For them it's just an empty space" (*Germania*, 53).

Wilson's reflections upon American audiences' responses to his own productions suggest that Müller is mistaken here. Explaining that he likes "a situation similar to the experience that one has when one is listening to a radio, when one can imagine pictures," where "there's a certain mental freedom or space for interior reflection, aurally and visually," Wilson, like Müller, asserts that it is his audience's job to read between the images and lines of his productions.

Rather than explicitly asking "Do you get it audience? Do you get it?" Wilson observes:

> I don't want to draw any conclusions, and I'd rather process it in time, as something we think about, that's a continuum. When the curtain goes down, you don't stop thinking about it. You go home and still think about it. It's part of an ongoing thing, it's a continuum, it's something that never, never finishes. It's something that continues to intrigue or fascinate. (interview with author, 5 Feb. 1991)

In this respect, Wilson argues that his work is no different to any other kind of significant theater:

> Why do we go back to *King Lear*? Because we can think about it in multiple ways. It has no one way of thinking about it. It cannot be interpreted. It could not be fully comprehended. So it's foolish for us to think that we can understand what it is that we're saying or doing. Because it's far too complex. But to assume that we can understand what it is we're doing is a lie. I feel that the author, the director, the actor, is assuming too much that he understands the situation, instead of approaching it with a more open mind. The question—*What is it that I'm saying?—What is it that I'm doing?* That's the reason

to make theatre. And if we have the answers, don't do it. There's no need to do it. (interview with author, 5 Feb. 1991)

Wilson also suggests that far from being exclusive to the avant-garde, the exploration of unpredictable juxtapositions is discernible in almost all art. In other words, rather than discerning a total, all-or-nothing rupture between orderly past modes of theater and disorderly modes of contemporary avant-garde theatre, Wilson affirms the continuity between past and present explorations of theme and variation.

Didn't artists always do that? Didn't Mozart do that, start with a theme and get a variation? Didn't Shakespeare do that? Didn't Euripedes? It's nothing new. It's one thing that artists do. Avant-garde is just rediscovering the classics, what we've already known. It's always the same patterns.[3]

In much the same way, Müller enthusiastically asserts his empathy for, and continuity with, the works of Shakespeare— "the human being I feel the closest to":

I experienced this when I translated *As You Like It* with the firm intention of changing nothing. It was as though I was working in his body. I developed a sense for the androgynous element, this mixture between snake and wildcat movements in his language, in the dramaturgy of his plays. Since then I have felt that I know him personally. (*Germania*, 210)

While this anecdote points to comparable "wildcat movements" in both Müller's and Shakespeare's work, Müller also makes the obvious point that Shakespeare's plays responded to quite different cultural "working conditions" and—as Eco might observe—to a quite distinctive period of historical transition (*Travels*, 84). Distinguishing between these circumstances, Müller comments, "We too are living in a transition stage today, but without tranquillity. In addition, there was no film, no television and no separation between high and popular art" (*Germania*, 211).

As these lines economically suggest, it is precisely the impact of new technologies, and of new mass-media modes of popular art, upon more conventional cultural traditions, that give postmodern creativity its distinctive transitional intensity and identity. Significantly, Müller's and Wilson's differing practices lend themselves to collaborative projects transcending the cultural barriers, walls, and paradigms of East and West. Equally telling, Müller and Wilson both suggest that their work simultaneously evinces discontinuity from their immediate precursors and continuity with theatrical traditions as a whole. These dynamic paradoxes indicate not so much the waning of the avant-garde in an era overwhelmed by the most pervasive and persuasive symptoms of the petrification of hope, as compelling evidence of the postmodern avant-garde's mature self-identification and self-assertion as an international creative force. Evincing both revolutionary and reconciliatory energies, the collaborations of Müller and Wilson challenge the B-effect convert to look beyond the banalities of mass culture toward the more rewarding innovations and initiatives of the nineties.

Notes

1. Robert Wilson, interview with author, 5 Feb. 1991. All subsequent references to this interview appear in the text.
2. Heiner Müller, "Müller on Wilson," trans. Stephan Meier, in the program for the American Repertory Theatre production of Müller's *Quartet*, Boston, A.R.T., 1988, unpaginated.
3. Robert Wilson, "Interview with Gary Susman," Robert Wilson issue of *Stuff Magazine* (Boston), February 1991, unpaginated.

Huyssen and the Endgame of the Avant-Garde ❑

Beuys's, Cage's, Eco's, Grass's, Carrington's, Wolf's, Müller's, and Wilson's enthusiasms for previous cultures—be these primitive, mythological, classical, shamanistic, folkloric, Oriental, North American, medieval, or contemporary variants of third world and underprivileged communities or contemporary revivals of the early twentieth century avant-garde's experiments—might all initially appear to be symptoms of what Andreas

Huyssen disapprovingly terms "the obnoxious nostalgia of the 1970's."[1] Discussing such collective symptoms as "nostalgia for Egyptian mummies (Tut exhibit in United States), medieval emperors (Stauffer exhibit in Stuttgart), or most recently, Vikings (Minneapolis)," Huyssen speculates that this widespread nostalgia confirms that "there seems to be little doubt that the classical avant-garde has exhausted its creative potential" and that "the waning of the avant-garde is widely acknowledged as a *fait accompli*" (*After the Great Divide*, 162).

While Huyssen acknowledges that some may associate this nostalgic impulse with "the promise of a revitalization in contemporary culture," he is more inclined to share the view that it indicates "the exhaustion of cultural resources and creativity in our own time" (*After the Great Divide*, 162). For Huyssen, then, the "recuperation of history" and the "re-emergence of the story in the 1970's" are not so much part of a productive, reconciliatory "leap back into a pre-modern, pre-avantgarde past" as "attempts to shift into reverse in order to get out of a dead-end street where the vehicle of avantgardism and postmodernism have come to a standstill" (174).

Like many B-effect theorists, Huyssen predictably concludes that both mainstream modernist experiments and modernism's classical avant-garde experiments offer little inspiration to the postmodern sensibility. Apparently, "too many aspects of the trajectory of modernity have become suspect and unviable today":

> Even the aesthetically and politically most fascinating components of modernity, the historical avantgarde, no longer offers solutions for major sections of contemporary culture, which would reject the avantgarde's universalizing and totalizing gesture as much as its ambiguous espousal of technology and modernization. (*After the Great Divide*, 175)

These comments leave Huyssen in a curious double bind. On the one hand, he asserts that the technological avant-garde is technically dead or at very least, unlikely to have any impact in postmodern America where "a technologically and economically fully developed media culture" has mastered "the high art of integrating, diffusing, and marketing even the most serious challenges," making "the shock of the new ... much harder, perhaps even impossible, to sustain" (168).

On the other hand, Huyssen clearly deplores the degree to which this same audience laps up the kind of kitsch nostalgia that Eco likewise dismisses as the superficial "constant 'past-izing' process carried out by American civilization in its alternate process of futuristic planning and nostalgic remorse" (*Travels*, 9–10).

The obvious objection to Huyssen's analysis is that it confuses the stupidities and superficialities of mass culture with the subtleties and substance of much of the postmodern avant-garde. In Huyssen's terms, there never could be an authentically postmodern avant-garde—be this primitive or technological—since both possibilities have been neutralized by mass culture's alternating *past-izing* and futuristic planning.

Combined with his more accurate observation that the American postmodern avant-garde is in many ways a compensation for "the absence of an indigenous American avant-garde in the classical, European sense, say in the 1930s" (*After the Great Divide*, 167), and with his questionable assumption that the classical European avant-garde was "liquidated culturally and politically by Stalin and Hitler" (168), Huyssen's excessive emphasis upon the insensitivity of American mass culture's audiences and his own apparent insensitivity to the international technological avant-garde's positive practices prompt his eventual suggestion that the American postmodern avant-garde is at best the *endgame* of its liquidated European modernist precursor. Huyssen misleadingly concludes,

> Despite its radical and legitimate critique of the gospel of modernism, postmodernism, which in its artistic practices and its theory was a product of the 1960's, must be seen as the endgame of the avant-garde and not as the radical breakthrough as it often claimed to be. (168)

Note

1. Andreas Huyssen, *After the Great Divide: Modernism, Mass Culture, Postmodernism* (Bloomington: Indiana Univ.

Press, 1986), 162. All subsequent references to this work appear in the text.

Huyssen, Popper, and the Electrification of the Avant-Garde ❏

As Huyssen notes, postmodern culture's nostalgic impulse surfaces more substantially within the social, political, and historical research that he associates with "alternative forms" and "minority" practices, such as

> the art, writing, film-making and criticism of women and minority artists with their recuperation of buried and mutilated traditions, their emphasis on exploring forms of gender-and race-based subjectivity in aesthetic productions and experiences, and their refusal to be limited to standard canonizations. (*After the Great Divide,* 198)

Ironically, Huyssen's vulnerability to the standard B-effect myth asserting the death of the historical and classical avant-gardes distracts him from the equally significant alternative forms of culture initiated by the many minority artists of the postmodern technological avant-garde. Huyssen's suggestion that the artistic practices and theories of postmodernism constitute a "dead-end" (174) and "deathmask" (168) culture peculiar to the sixties is best reconsidered in terms of the technological tradition documented by Frank Popper in his 1983 exhibition *Electra* at the *Musée d'Art Moderne* in Paris.

As Popper's *Electra Chronologie* demonstrates, the last half-century witnesses continual breakthroughs in the emerging postmodern fields of electronic and kinetic art. Significantly, this chronology not only focuses predominantly upon Eastern and Western European experiments in the late modernist years (1913 to1935) but also documents increasing international innovations, exhibitions, and collaborations in the postmodern years (1936 to the present) as artists in Europe, Asia, North

America, and South America concurrently reacted to the creative potential of their era's new technologies.

It is perhaps worth emphasizing that after the mid-fifties, Popper's data escalates across truly cosmopolitan frontiers, recording exhibitions in Buenos Aires, Paris, Zurich, Vienna (1956); New York and Rotterdam (1957); Frankfurt, Brussels, Paris (1958); Paris, Dusseldorf, Weisbaden, Milan, Cologne, New York (1959); Paris, Buenos Aires, New York, Zurich, Cologne (1960); Amsterdam, Tokyo, New York (1961); and Buenos Aires, Moscow, Bâle, Antwerp, Amsterdam, London (1962)—to cite only the years between the mid-fifties and the beginning of the sixties.

Huyssen's hypothesis that postmodern artistic practices and theory are both products of the sixties and—geographically and chronologically speaking—the American endgame of the European twenties requires reconsideration. As Frank Popper demonstrates, postmodern culture's quintessentially technological innovations offer innumerable international additions to—and radical breakthroughs from—the continuing tradition of the European modernist avant-garde's explorations of kinetic and electronic art. The following extracts from Popper's chronology sketch a few of the landmarks in this virtually century-long tradition.[1]

1913 Duchamp's *Bicycle Wheel*
       Tatlin's first suspended relief
1914 Balla's and Depero's first mobiles
1915 Gabo's first constructions
1916 Baranoff-Rossine patents his electronic *Opto-Phonic Piano*
1917 Rodchenko's metal mobiles
1918 Pfenninger's sonic writing
1919 Eggeling's and Richter's abstract scrolls
1920 Montalti's *Electro-vibro-luminous* theater
       Gabo's first kinetic sculptures
1921 Hirschfeld-Mack's *Reflected Colour Displays*
1922 Duchamp's *Rotor-Relief*
1923 Braun's *Luminous-Electric Sculptures*
1924 Wilfred patents his projection systems

1925	Prampolini's *Magnetic Theatre* project
1926	Klein publishes *Colour Music*
	Lye makes first drawings on film
1927	Schlemmer's Bauhaus light project
1928	Tchelitchew designs neon and cinematographic set for Nabokoff's ballet *Ode*
1929	Marinetti's play *Rapid Lights*
	Wilfred's *Mural Mobile*
	Gabo's *Light Festival*
1930	Pesanek exhibits *Female Torsos* surrounded by neon
1931	Man Ray's *Electricité*
1932	Calder's *Mobiles*
	Pesanek's color organ
1933	Munari's *Useless Machine*
1935	Moholy-Nagy's *Space-Light-Modulator*
	Lye's *Colourbox*
1936	Moholy-Nagy publishes *Vom Pigment zum Farblicht*
1938	Cage's *Bacchanale*
	Vasarely experiments with mobiles
	Munari publishes *Macchina d'Arte*
1940	Prampolini's *Electric Pavilion*
	Cage's *Living Room Music*
1941	Pesanek publishes *Kinetismus*
1944	Kepes publishes *Language of Vision*
	Mortensen constructs *Kinetic Picture*
1945	Rickey's first mobiles
	Wilfred's *Lumia* compositions
	Kosice founds *Arte Concreta-Invencion* group in Buenos Aires
1946	Kosice exhibits neon sculptures
	Fontana publishes *Manifesto Blanco*
1947	Moholy-Nagy publishes *Vision in Motion*
1948	Schoffer's first *spatiodynamique* works
	Tinguely's first mechanical sculptures
1949	Rickey's first glass kinetic sculptures
	Fontana's ultraviolet light environment
1950	Palatnik's cine-chromatic machines
	Lassus's *Visuelles Farbambiente*
1951	Fontana's neon drawings
1952	Agam develops transformable images
	Cage's *Silence*

	First happening at Black Mountain College
	Laposky's *Electronic Abstractions*
1953	Tinguely's *Métamechanisme*
	Bury's *Plans Mobiles*
	Schoffer's *Spectacle lumino-dynamique*
1954	Schoffer's *Tour Spatiodynamique*
	Tinguely's *Relief métamecanique sonore* and *Machine à dessiner*

Huyssen is certainly persuasive when he argues that the main tendency in mainstream West German culture in the sixties was a rediscovery of "moderns who had been burnt and banned during the Third Reich" (*After the Great Divide*, 190). By contrast, his parallel suggestion that France similarly witnessed "a return to modernism rather than a step beyond it" (191) pivots embarrassingly upon the very evidence that it discredits.

According to Huyssen, French theory "provides us primarily with an *archeology of modernity*, a theory of modernism at the stage of its exhaustion," rather than "an analysis of contemporary culture" (*After the Great Divide*, 209). This is precisely what Huyssen does when discussing French postmodern culture in terms of French theory rather than in terms of the various technological innovations documented by Popper's *Electra-Chronologie*.

To base one's assessment of French postmodern creativity upon French poststructuralist theory is like studying postmodern American theater on the basis of Ronald Reagan's collected speeches. As the poet and artist Brion Gysin intimates in a letter angrily concluding "Fuck the intertextualists!"[2] poststructuralist—and intertextual—theory seems alarmingly indifferent toward innovative contemporary creativity. Baudrillard, for example, boasts that he is happy to remain a foreigner before media art. "When I'm watching the screen I'm more or less a pure spectator. . . . It's a foreign domain, and I want to retain this foreign quality. I want to remain a foreigner there."[3]

Huyssen similarly seems to be at least partially a foreigner in the realm of the new electronic media. At times, he dismisses their potential with allusions to his suspicion that television is "pollution rather than panacea" (*After the Great Divide*, 196) and that technological enthusiasms are "more a symptom of the disease than a cure" (173). On other occasions, he attempts to distinguish the conceptual impact of feminist art from the aspirations of technological art by making oversimplistic distinctions between "feminist interest in women's history and the ecological search for alternatives in our relationship with nature" and "logocentric and technocratic thought" (172).

Either way, Huyssen tends to overlook the many instances in which effective feminist critiques of logocentric thought and ecological irresponsibility depend upon the new technologies of the eighties and the nineties. As Jenny Holzer suggests, "It's important, since we live in an age where there are so many technological marvels and horrors, to use technology when appropriate. If high tech gets the message across, it would be stupid to turn your back on it."[4] Likewise, as the performance artist Diamanda Galas rather more menacingly comments, electronic art may well seem most significant as a means by which women artists transcend logocentric or lethargic minimalism.

> There is a stupid concept that electronics have us evolving to this unfeeling inhuman state. I dominate my electronics. When the equipment is not working I keep trying, doing it. . . . I get angry. I do not put myself to sleep with music. I hate minimal crap. My music is maximal. I hate that dead shit![5]

Huyssen's final suggestion that "the postmodern . . . simultaneously delimits and opens our horizons" and is thus "our problem and our hope" (*After the Great Divide*, 221) is certainly more diplomatic than his prevailing insistence upon the general decline or death of the postmodern avant-garde.

Notes

1. The following chronology represents a very liberal summary of the much more detailed *Electra Chronologie* in the catalog for Frank Popper's exhibition, *Electra: Electricity and Electronics in the Art of the XXth Century* (Paris: Musée d'Art Moderne de la Ville de Paris, 1983), 83–111. My summaries and my translation. I am referring in some detail to this important

chronology in order to clarify the consistently neglected *continuity* between the modernist and postmodern technological avantgarde traditions.

2. Brion Gysin, letter to the author, 24 Sept. 1984.

3. Jean Baudrillard, "Fractal Theory: Baudrillard and the Contemporary Arts," interview with author, *Paragraph* 13.3 (Nov. 1990): 288.

4. Jenny Holzer, "Interview with Nicholas Zurbrugg" (1991), *Eyeline* (Brisbane), no. 16 (Spring 1991): 21. All subsequent references to this interview appear in the text.

5. Diamanda Galas, "I dominate my electronics," interview with Carl Heyward, *Art Com*, no. 22 (1983): 23.

Buñuel, Breton, Benjamin, Baudrillard, and the Myths of Mechanical Depersonalization ❏

Modernist and postmodernist experiments with the new filmic mass media provoke four main responses: aesthetic enthusiasm, aesthetic nihilism, critical neutrality, and critical inanity.

Writing in his "Notes on the Making of *Un Chien Andalou*," Luis Buñuel distinguishes this film of 1929 from the earlier avant-garde cinema of "Ruttmann, Cavalcanti, Man Ray, Dziga Verloff, René Clair, Dulac, Ivens, etc.," on the grounds that

> historically, this film represents a violent reaction against what was at that time called "avantgarde cine," which was directed exclusively to the artistic sensibility and to the reason of the spectator with its play of light and shadow, its photographic effects, its preoccupation with rhyme montage and technical research, and at times in the direction of this display of a perfectly conventional and reasonable mind.[1]

Claiming that his film draws inspiration from "poetry, freed from the ballast of reason," in order "to provoke . . . instinctive reactions of attraction and of repulsion," Buñuel concludes that "rational, esthetic or . . . technical matters" are irrelevant." *Un*

Chien Andalou . . . has no intention of attracting nor pleasing the spectator; indeed on the contrary, it attacks him, to the degree that he belongs to a society with which surrealism is at war" ("Notes," 152).

The immediate public acclaim greeting this film forced Buñuel to adopt still more desperate rhetoric. Accused by Aragon of "suspect . . . commercial success" and confronted by Breton's question, "Are you with the police or with us?" Buñuel volunteered to "burn the negative . . . something I would have done without hesitation had the group agreed."[2] In his preface to the film's scenario in *La Révolution Surréaliste* (1929), Buñuel once again denied that he had ever aspired to create a successful film, complaining, "But what can I do about people who are crazy for anything new, even if the novelty outrages their inmost convictions."[3]

Like Buñuel, Huyssen similarly asserts that bourgeois culture's capacity to "co-opt any kind of attack made on it" renders such attacks unsuccessful (*After the Great Divide*, 147)—an assertion assuming that aggressive avant-garde art axiomatically aspires to remain permanently aggressive. According to this logic, *co-option* by society implies neutralization. On the contrary, it could be argued that the assimilation of dadaist or surrealist concepts signals the conceptual *invasion* of the public sensibility and the triumphant institutionalization of innovative ideas (somewhat like the departmental legitimation of the deconstructive avant-garde in the seventies and the eighties).

Undue emphasis upon the apparently unavoidable neutrality of popular or successful experimentation, particularly mass-media experimentation, leads in turn to Benjamin's confusing hypothesis that mechanically reproduced art axiomatically loses all sense of personal aura. This in turn provokes Baudrillard's more recent nihilistic hypothesis that film, video, and television in particular are not merely neutral, postauratic media but are neutralizing, post*everything* media, sapping the average powers of the average sensibility in much the same way that kryptonite zaps the super powers of Superman. Pondering upon the lowest common denominator of the mass impact of mass media upon mass audiences, Baudrillard defines the screen as an alarmingly reductive medium that "makes everything circulate in one space without depth, where all the objects must be able to follow one after the other without slowing down or stopping the circuit."[4]

If modernist writers and critics like to emphasize the "bombardment" of images, postmoderns such as Baudrillard seem especially fond of the more animated concept of "circulating" images. Updated for reconsumption in the nineties, the structuralist sixties' myth of the printed text's depthless neutrality returns in the guise of the poststructuralist fiction of the filmic text's invariably impersonal superficiality.

Consolidating this fiction, Jameson's essay "Reading Without Interpretation: Postmodernism and the Video-Text" (1987) denounces video as "a ceaseless rotation of elements such that they change place at every moment, with the result that no single element can occupy the position of 'interpretant' (or that of primary sign) for any length of time" and addends Baudrillard's extravagant discovery of "the dissolution of life into TV" with the still more bizarre warning that once exposed to the mechanical *depersonalization* of the new medium, "auteurs themselves are dissolved along with the spectator" (205).

It is perhaps more accurate to argue that unrestrained enthusiasm for the rhetoric of mechanical depersonalization dissolves multimedia *life* into B-effect theory.

Notes

1. Luis Buñuel, "Notes on the Making of *Un Chien Andalou*," in *The World of Luis Buñuel*, ed. Joan Mellen (New York: Oxford Univ. Press, 1978), 151. All subsequent references to this work appear in the text.

2. Luis Buñuel, *My Last Breath*, trans. Abigail Israel (Glasgow: Flamingo, 1985), 108, 110.

3. Luis Buñuel, scenario from *Un Chien Andalou* (1929), in *Luis Buñuel: An Introduction*, by Ado Kyrou (New York: Simon and Schuster, 1963), 142.

4. Jean Baudrillard, "The Work of Art in the Electronic Age," interview, trans. Lucy Forsyth, *Block*, no. 14 (Autumn 1988): 9.

DeLillo, Müller, Lyotard, Kroker, and the Panic Sensibility ☐

As Don DeLillo suggests in *White Noise* (1984), mass-cultural artifacts frequently serve a doubly delusory function. On the one hand, publications such as the *National Enquirer* vulgarize the spiritual by offering a "weekly dose of cult mysteries" (5) to audiences who turn to tabloid pages for "everything that we need that is not food or love. . . . The tales of the supernatural and the extraterrestrial. The miracle vitamins, the cures for cancer, the remedies for obesity. The cults of the famous and the dead" (326).

At the other extreme, *White Noise* parodies the way in which excessive emphasis upon the icons of consumer culture precipitates the vulgarity and aridity of "movie-mad, trivia-crazed" professors of popular culture who "read nothing but cereal boxes" because these constitute "the only avant-garde we've got" (9–10).

The irony here, of course, is that the very academics who detect the dissolution of reality, the death of the subject, and the decline of the avant-garde in the movie-mad, trivia-crazed fabric of postmodern society are themselves virtually movie-mad, trivia-crazed, and indifferent to anything other than what they consider "the natural language of the culture" (*White Noise*, 9).

As Heiner Müller forcefully argues, there is nothing innocent or natural about the languages of the mass media. Reflecting upon the brutalizing impact of Japanese television cartoons, Müller observes:

> In Italy one sees children who spend up to seven hours daily in front of the television set watching Japanese cartoons, in comparison to which the American cartoons have Faustian depth and a great humanistic content, since they still have some remains of humour, whereas the Japanese films are as stupid as they are brutal. After the children have been watching these cartoons for several months or years, all they will ever be capable of is what the market demands of them. (*Germania*, 186)

Ignoring the demands of what Huyssen terms "major sections of contemporary culture" (*After the Great Divide*, 175), Müller suggests that the most reliable antidote to such brutalizing modes of mass culture are the more or less minority writings that he associates with potentially permanent "Poetic Information":

> For this reason what I write must be as permanent as possible, regardless of the fact that in East Germany my plays are always produced fifteen years after they are written. This is a good discipline. I must not create disposable literature. From the moment one accepts that there will be no future generation, there will be no more quality. (*Germania*, 213)

This is precisely what the postmodern panic mentality accepts when it argues, like Jameson, that "there are no more masterpieces, no more great books" or when it attempts, like Baudrillard, to analyze *America* in terms of "the zero degree of culture" or proposes, like Lyotard, to diagnose the *Postmodern Condition* in terms of "the degree zero of contemporary culture" (76).[1] At best, such trivia-crazed analysis leads to the kind of theoretical fiction that Lyotard fabricates in his much quoted invention of the jet-setting, "kitsch-person," for whom "knowledge is a matter of TV games," who "listens to reggae, watches a western, eats McDonald's food for lunch and local cuisine for dinner, wears Paris perfume in Tokyo and 'retro' clothes in Hong Kong" (76).

At worst, this kitsch-oriented approach to postmodern culture leads to the *Panic Encyclopedia* compiled by Arthur Kroker, Marilouise Kroker, and David Cook.[2] A "definitive guide" to such aspects of the postmodern scene as panic doughnuts, panic Elvis, panic history, and panic hamburgers, this volume characteristically identifies "*Postmodern hamburgers* . . . Hamburgers which have been aestheticized to such a point of frenzy and hysteria that the McDonalds hamburger has actually vanished into its own sign" (118).

The subsequent *panic* conclusion that "McDonald's is a perfect technological hologram of suburban America and of its extension by the capillaries of highways across the nation"

(*Panic Encyclopedia*, 118) has much in common with the dated apocalyptic rhetoric of the science fiction novelist J. G. Ballard's *Atrocity Exhibition* (1970), a work that equates seams between sections of "a motorway extension" with "the sutures of an exposed skull."[3]

Like the TV evangelist Jim Bakker (discussed under the heading "Panic God"), the *Panic Encyclopedia* authors seem well aware that "in America, you have to be excessive to be successful" (113). Ironically, as Ballard himself now intimates, it seems a little late in the day to be fabricating literary and theoretical counterparts to the "sensational imagery that emerged from our TV screens" in the sixties.[4]

Notes

1. Jameson, "Reading Without Interpretation," 208; Baudrillard, *America*, 78.

2. Arthur Kroker, Marilouise Kroker, David Cook, *Panic Encyclopedia: The Definitive Guide to the Postmodern Scene* (London: MacMillan, 1989). All subsequent references to this work appear in the text.

3. J. G. Ballard, *The Atrocity Exhibitions*, rev. ed. (San Francisco: Re/Search, 1990), 31. All subsequent references to this novel and to Ballard's annotations to this novel refer to this edition and appear in the text.

4. J. G. Ballard, qtd. in "Riverside Demons," by Andrew Billen, *Observer* (London), 15 Sept. 1991, 62.

Ballard, The Kindness of Women, *and Catharsis* ◻

J. G. Ballard's own most recent writings typify the way in which many of the more interesting writers and artists of the sixties and seventies have now transcended what the Krokers might term the "panic" mentality. On the one hand, Ballard explains that his bafflement before the "complete discontinuity ... between Reagan's manner and body language ... and his scarily simplistic far-right message" led him to write *Atrocity Exhibition*'s consciously obscene fragment "Why I Want to Fuck Ronald Reagan," a pseudoclinical documentation of the incidence of "powerful erotic fantasies of an anal-sadistic character" in patients exposed to images of Reagan in "a series of simulated autocrashes, e.g., multiple pile-ups, head-on collisions, motorcade attacks" (105). At a general, polemical level, Ballard's more recent writings such as his annotations for the revised edition of *Atrocity Exhibition* (1990) still advocate "more sex and violence on TV, not less," claiming that "both are powerful catalysts for change in areas where change is overdue" (74). Significantly, the predominantly autobiographical rhetoric of his most recent novel, *The Kindness of Women* (1991), refreshingly renounces "powerful catalysts" in favor of more modest "catharsis."[1]

Something of the change in direction of Ballard's vision in this novel becomes evident in its very copyright details, where Ballard affirmatively insists upon his own creative identity, claiming "the moral right to be identified as the author of this work" (*Kindness of Women*, 4). Attaining, and then asserting, a similar sense of self-knowledge and self-sufficiency after witnessing a "masterly" filmic "recreation" (284) of his childhood in wartime Shanghai, the novel's narrator seems to recover from his erstwhile panic mentality and concludes,

> The time of desperate strategems was over, the car crashes and the hallucinogens, the deviant sex ransacked like a library of extreme metaphors. . . . The happiness I had found had been waiting for me within the modest reach of my own arms, in my children and the women I had loved, and in my friends who had made their own way through the craze years. (285)

The narrator's further recognition that film is the positive catalyst introducing "the last act in a profound catharsis that had taken decades to draw to a close" (284) and the suggestion that the "replica of a replica" of "Heyerdahl's papyrus ship— *Ra*" is probably still more "seaworthy than Heyerdahl's original" (285) additionally reinforce the extent to which *Kindness of Women* makes a clean break with the earlier, more pessimistic,

Ballardian stories, prompting Jameson's recent suggestion that their author is "one of the greatest postcontemporary dystopians."[2]

A major exception to Jameson's continued claim that Ballard's work offers a monument to "the pathos of entropy," where "what is mourned is the memory of deep memory; what is enacted is a nostalgia for nostalgia, for the grand older extinct questions of origins and telos" (*Postmodernism*, 156), *Kindness of Women* suggests that Ballard is now best described as one of the great contemporary *ex-dystopians*.

Discussing Baudrillard's *America*, for example, Ballard tellingly comments, "He takes an optimistic view of America and I would do the same about the world as a whole."[3] Perhaps Ballard's decades-long quest for catharsis is finally most noteworthy in terms of the ways in which it intimates that fiction—and theory, perhaps—may eventually extricate themselves from the panic mythologies of the craze years.

Notes

1. J. G. Ballard, *The Kindness of Women* (London: Harper Collins, 1991), 284. All subsequent references to this work appear in the text.

2. Fredric Jameson, *Postmodernism, or, The Cultural Logic of Late Capitalism* (Durham: Duke Univ. Press, 1991), 385. All subsequent references to this work appear in the text.

3. J. G. Ballard, interview with the author, 8 Jan. 1992.

Beyond the Disappearance of Value: Anderson and Acker ❑

One of the most curious tendencies of the postmodern eighties is the way in which cultural theorists compete with one another to evoke ever more startling descriptions of the supposedly schizophrenic sensibility that Jameson associates with "isolated, disconnected, discontinuous material signifiers which fail to link up into a coherent sequence" and that the Krokers in turn describe as "the catastrophic, because fun, implosion of America into a whole series of panic scenes."[1]

The undisputed master of such apocalyptic fiction is undoubtedly Baudrillard. As he admits,

> My way of reflecting on things is not dialectic. Rather it's provocative, reversible, it's a way of raising a thing to their "N"th power . . . a way of following through the extremes to see what happens. It's a bit like a theory-fiction. There's a little theoretical science fiction in it.[2]

Baudrillard equates the eighties with the extreme confusion that Hollywood might dub *Schizophrenia II*. Apparently, we witness

> a new form of schizophrenia . . . less the loss of the real . . . as is commonly said: but very much to the contrary, the absolute proximity, the total instantaneity of things, the feeling of no defence, no retreat . . . the end of interiority and intimacy, the overexposure and transparence of the world which traverses (the schizo) without obstacle.[3]

Raising this hypothetical vertigo to its nth power, Baudrillard concludes by suggesting that this *new* form of schizophrenia immobilizes all the faculties, so that the schizo, the artist, or the postmodern individual *per se* "can no longer produce the limits of his being, can no longer play nor stage himself, can no longer produce himself as a mirror . . . [and] is now only a pure screen, a switching centre for all the networks of influence."[4]

When considered overliterally, Baudrillard's splendidly exaggerated speculations may become as misleading as they are entertaining. What strikes one time after time when considering the recent work of American postmoderns is their unambiguous assertion and demonstration that they *can* "play," "stage," and "produce" works that mirror the limits of their experience.

The American performance artist Laurie Anderson, for example, insists that the fragments, the inferences, the suggestions, and the "snatches of conversation" in her performances all cohere in an artistic whole: "I don't think of them as fragments. I think of them as parts of a picture. . . . I don't think a

145

work of art is totally completed unless someone sees it and the transfer is made."[5]

Like Cage, Anderson suggests that her collage narratives offer an alternative mode of communication and perception to linear discourse rather than an absence or a negation of the communicative impulse.

> That's why I'm not a pamphleteer—I'm an artist. I like colour and sound. It makes me respond to something in a particular way. If I was just interested in what things meant, if I was just some kind of reductionist French philosopher, I would really just write it down and xerox it, and hand it out. I would not bother to go to all this trouble of turning these words into colours, and colours back into words and notes, and finding the right tone of voice to say things in.[6]

Far from accepting the prevalent panic logic of much post-modern theory, Anderson concludes,

> But for anyone to say that creativity is dead just says that this particular person is creatively dead. Until we're all dead, creativity isn't dead. It changes, and I think that a lot of people can't identify what it means, because they're looking for it in the wrong place. (interview with author, 30 Jan. 1991)

The American novelist Kathy Acker makes much the same point. While she acknowledges that French poststructuralist theory provided "a way to understand why I was writing the way I was," Acker—like Anderson—rejects the reductive, destructive, apocalyptic impulse in B-effect theory.

> I have trouble with Baudrillard's work. . . . When he writes that "there's no more value, there's only this black hole," I find this denial almost a celebration of—if you want to call it that—the disappearance of value. I find this celebration very problematic because the way it's been interiorized in this culture, it becomes a celebration of consumerism and of the kind of culture we've got and this I dislike greatly. I mean, I don't think to say that we want to get rid of the centralized phallus as the main structure around which we all turn, or that we want to get rid of the Oedipal myth as the main structure of this society, is a way of saying we want no values.[7]

Acker finally suggests that writers and artists may look beyond the seduction of theoretical debates and "work positively" rather than "against." For example, discussing her reaction to an invitation to respond to a panelist advocating "feminist anti-pornography," Acker comments,

> I said, "Why don't we talk about something positive? I don't care any more about people who are arguing against pornography. They're boring—I've been through the arguments five million times. Let's talk about something a lot of women in San Francisco who are in different fields are working on very positively—female sexuality, what the female body is, images of female sexuality, what women really desire." (interview with author, 8 June 1991)

Notes

1. Fredric Jameson, "Post-Modernism and Consumer Society," in *The Anti-Aesthetic*, 119. Arthur and Marilouise Kroker, "Panic Sex in America," in *Body Invaders: Sexuality and the Postmodern Condition*, ed. Arthur and Marilouise Kroker (London: Macmillan, 1988), 17.

2. Jean Baudrillard, "Game with Vestiges," interview with Salvatore Mele and Mark Titmarch, *On the Beach* (Sydney), no. 5 (Winter 1984): 20.

3. Baudrillard, "The Ecstasy of Communication," 132–33.

4. Baudrillard, "The Ecstasy of Communication," 133.

5. Laurie Anderson, "Speaking in Tongues," interview with Barbara Lehmann, *Performance Magazine*, no. 41 (May/June 1986): 12.

6. Laurie Anderson, interview with author, 30 Jan. 1991. All subsequent references to this interview appear in the text.

7. Kathy Acker, interview with author, 8 June 1991. All subsequent references to this interview appear in the text.

Toward Effective Communication:
Kruger and Holzer ❏

Responding slightly more enthusiastically to Baudrillard's writings than Kathy Acker, the feminist photographic and language artist Barbara Kruger suggests that Baudrillard "has been prescient in understanding the power of television . . . he's written very clearly about the narcoleptic effect of the media—of its power to transfix and freeze."[1]

Whereas Acker places her work within the "poète maudite lineage" that she associates with artists like Burroughs who "posit themselves as being *against* the ongoing society and culture" and who argue that "a society without dreams, without art . . . is a dead society" (interview with author, 8 June 1991), Kruger rather more pragmatically insists upon her social formation, stipulating, "I am not *not* a part of that society. I'm very much a part of it and have been constructed by that society" (interview with author, 19 June 1991).

Kruger identifies her main concern as the attempt to problematize the ways in which "people are no longer aware of how power is working in society . . . of how their lives are constructed and who is constructing them," and she associates her practice with "finding and asking questions that might help to discover different ways to think of life—to think of a way to perceive, or to think of a process, that's not based on binary oppositions" (interview with author, 19 June 1991).

While Kruger deplores mass film culture—"there are six movies playing in this country today, most of which are crappy"—she nevertheless argues that mass culture may still be used productively by artists willing to displace conventional expectations. Considering the potential of television, Kruger argues that rather than remaining "in some art ghetto where my work is broadcast on TV as 'art,' " she would prefer to write sit-coms and thereby "be in the system and change the narrative positioning of the work that you see on it." In brief, Kruger's objective is to "struggle in the sites that we can begin to be effective on" (interview with author, 19 June 1991).

Exactly the same emphasis upon effective, credible, public practices informs the work of Kruger's fellow language artist, Jenny Holzer. Explaining that she wishes to "make some alternative pronouncements," Holzer places her work in the context of "political posters and broadcasts" ("Interview with Zurbrugg," 21). Like Kruger's verbal-visual montages, Holzer's early work, *The Truisms*, avoided overexplicit arguments by listing "all the ways of thinking about things," a strategy some viewers criticized for its ideological imprecision. Holzer now accepts this criticism, acknowledging that "there are pressing problems that need immediate solutions" (19).

Most interesting here is Holzer's wish to find immediate solutions to pressing problems. Like Kruger, she has also contemplated television as a public medium, infiltrating the familiar with the unfamiliar. Holzer suggests that her public service announcements succeeded not so much as self-conscious artworks as pieces "close enough to what normally appears on television to be credible" ("Interview with Zurbrugg," 20). In other words, Holzer, like Kruger, focuses explicitly upon processes of public conditioning, fighting fire as it were with fire, by employing the mass media to articulate "the usual themes, the survival themes," "to highlight some issues, to try to make the problems that actually are here seem real to people all over again" (21).

Note

1. Barbara Kruger, interview with author, 19 June 1991. All subsequent references to this interview appear in the text.

Appropriation, Neutralization, and
Reconciliation: Tillers and Johnson □

As Baudrillard himself acknowledges, excessive emphasis upon his theories has precipitated the rather predictable recycling of popular images that he associates with *simulationist* painting. Baudrillard refers here to "the 'simulationist' paint ers in New York" for whom the neutralizing process of banal appropriation "is taken for granted as something which they're happy to reproduce."[1]

The same unfortunate impulse informs the argument—if not the work—of Australian artists such as the painter Imants Tillers, who concludes that Australian art is inevitably parasitic upon bad reproductions devoid of aura, truth, or profundity. Developing this thesis Tillers explains,

> In Australia it is widely accepted that art has come to us secondhand through reproductions but hitherto this has been considered as a disadvantage—an unfortunate by-product of our physical and cultural isolation. Now we are beginning to recognize this as an advantage. We have been protected from "originals,"—from their "aura," their surface and their authority. Furthermore the dot-screen of mechanical reproduction has rendered all images equivalent, interchangeable, scaleless and surface-less: for the Australian artist it has made art in the reproduced form the perfect material for *bricolage*.[2]

Tillers's emphasis upon the equivalent and interchangeable quality of such *bricolage* materials leads to the art critic Daniel Thomas's suggestion that the Australian artist, like the odious Bart Simpson, may well be fated to boast "underachiever and proud of it." In Thomas's terms, "At the end of the world . . . the flood of second-hand images is a welcome fact of life, to be exploited cheerfully and naturally. . . . There is none of the furtiveness with which nineteenth-century painters might have appropriated low-art images."[3]

Unlike Tillers and Thomas, the Sydney artist Tim Johnson suggests that reproductions of work from other cultures may be used substantially rather than superficially. Describing the consequences of appropriating—and combining—Aboriginal and Chinese images alongside the imagery of his own paintings, Johnson relates,

> It led to identifying myself as an Australian artist in that I was starting to see Australia as part of Asia instead of as part of Europe. I looked at a lot of Tibetan art which tied in with practising Buddhism and that allowed me to get into the theory behind making images—wherein you are invoking something. The theory allowed me to understand Aboriginal art better, because if you paint an Aboriginal design that has a link with the Dreamtime, the design summons up the Ancestor and the ancestral force involved in the event being portrayed. In the same way, if you paint a Buddha, the Buddha acts in your life or in other people's lives.[4]

Most significant here is Johnson's emphasis upon artistic quotation as a source of self-discovery, as a source of national and international identity, and even as a source of potential future events invoked by the artist.

This willing suspension of theoretical disbelief and this openness to other cultures and other terms of reference exemplify the most positive potential of the present postmodern sensibility. As Cage suggests, the simplistic internationalism of "the Pizza Hut in Moscow" is complemented by the more substantial global empathy of an optimism that comes from "awareness that we live on the same globe," "keeping the differences," and "eliminating power differences."[5]

Put another way, more than ever before, postmodern culture witnesses the positive denationalization—or internationalization—envisaged by Robert Wilson when outlining his projects for the nineties. Affirming his intentions to continue traveling, Wilson observes,

> I'm interested in working internationally. I've worked in Germany in the last three years and I'm trying to work more in Latin America and South America. That interests me. I'm going to do a piece in Caracas—I'm going to do a piece in Mexico, Buenos Aires and Brazil—a piece in Spain, and another in Portugal. I'm interested in Thailand, I'm very interested in going to Indonesia. I've worked in Japan, but I'd like

to go more into the roots of that culture. (interview with author, 5 Feb. 1991)

Notes

1. Baudrillard, "Fractal Theory," 286.
2. Imants Tillers, "The Paradox of Dick Watkins," in *Dick Watkins* (1985 São Paulo Bienal catalog) (Broken Hill, Australia: Broken Hill City Art Gallery), 11.
3. Daniel Thomas, "Dick Watkins and the Flood of Art," in *Dick Watkins*, 6.
4. Tim Johnson, interview with author, *Art and Australia* 29.1 (Spring 1991): 48.
5. John Cage, interview with author, 12 Sept. 1990.

Independent Internationalism: Finlay and Lax ❑

As Frank Popper's research on kinetic art indicates, the communications revolution of the postmodern period has often shifted the center of avant-garde movements from national capitals to the studios and studies of an international array of artists. In turn, the careers of the Scottish concrete poet Ian Hamilton Finlay and the American visual poet Robert Lax indicate the ways in which contemporary communications allow those leading the reclusive lives that Francesco Conz associates with "modern-day saints" (qtd. in Martin, 114) to participate both nationally and internationally in the fields of postmodern literature and art.

Emerging from and around an isolated Scottish farmhouse, Finlay's typographical and three-dimensional language works are most significant as compositions that *honor* past models of equanimity and integrity. Finlay's admiration for neoclassical order and austerity is evident in such works as *Homage to Malevich* (1963), a textual square reading "black block," in which he aligns himself with the suprematist project as an

152

artist interested in depicting "a model, of order, even if set in a space which is full of doubt."[1]

Off the page, Finlay's poems on wood and stone consciously evoke the perennial cycles of nature rather than the vertigo of urban and theoretical fashions. *Bring Back the Birch* is at once Finlay's homage to the order of the seasons and wry allusion to this pro–corporal punishment slogan. In other works Finlay attempted to translate his admiration for classical evocations of heroism into the contemporary iconography of his *Garden Temple* dedicated to "Apollo, His Music, His Missiles, His Muses."

When requested to pay commercial art gallery rates for this installation, Finlay refused to do so, arguing that his *Garden Temple* was quite literally a temple to art and beauty and as such a religious building, exempt from rates. Noting that his local taxmasters refused to accept the term *Garden Temple* because it was not on their computer program, Finlay comments that this dispute primarily pivots upon the question of "whether the spirit has any place in the world."[2] Finlay's appropriation and visual resurrection of the concept of the temple typifies his ongoing commitment to precisely the kind of deep ethical and metaphysical values that postmodern mass-media logic and parochial bureaucratic logic both deny.

This battle inspired Finlay to create a number of still more militant works combining references to Apollo, German military armament, and French revolutionary rhetoric. Employing images of Panzer tanks as contemporary emblems of terror, Finlay was subsequently charged with Nazi sympathies, an accusation leading to the cancellation of his invitation to design a garden celebrating the French Revolution for its bicentennial ceremonies. For all its tribulations, Finlay's experience reveals the ways in which contemporary art can appropriate, translate, and *reanimate* ethical values, irrespective of geographical location.

The poetry and general philosophy of Robert Lax affirm a similar sense of the compatibility and continuity between the most avant-garde and the most classical forms of creativity. Like Finlay, Lax has lived in almost total obscurity so far as mainstream recognition is concerned, composing meditative, abstract poems on the Greek islands of Kalymnos and Patmos. According to Lax, such islands offer a synthesis of past and present and allow the poet to discover ideal correspondences between "inner and outer worlds."

> I think this idea of a classical landscape has helped me clarify my thinking; I like being in a place where there is sea and sky and mountains, trees, even olive trees, and sheep and goats, shepherds. These are things which are natural, sacral, ancient, really classical and which have formed a great deal of the symbolism, the traditional symbolism, of western poetry.[3]

Lax's argument is that the very environment of the Greek islands permits a sense of communion with the poetic profundity of previous epochs and that this sense of communion points in turn to a more universal, timeless quality of perception. Looking beyond the provincial to more universal modes of consciousness Lax concludes,

> I think that any kind of provincialism in art may be . . . helpful at a certain stage of the game, but eventually, and naturally, later it can be dispensed with. Every nation and every village may have its own customs, but the customs that have the most meaning in art may be those that are most universal. (*New York Quarterly*, 27)

Like Finlay, Lax indicates that geographical isolation may prove a positive advantage to artists wishing to distill a more or less *universal* art from elements of inner and outer experience. Rather than responding literally to the outer world by deconstructing, denigrating, or celebrating the fairly obvious limitations of mass culture, Lax, like Finlay, Johnson, Monk, Wilson, and Cage, asserts the artist's capacity to reconcile and regenerate different cultural, geographical, temporal, and personal terms of reference.

Notes

1. Ian Hamilton Finlay, "Letter to Pierre Garnier, September 17th, 1963," *Hispanic Arts* 1.3–4 (Winter/Spring 1968): 84.

See also Yves Abrioux, *Ian Hamilton Finlay: A Visual Primer* (Edinburgh: Reaktion, 1985).

    2. Ian Hamilton Finlay, *Sunday Times* (London), 7 Aug. 1973.

    3. Robert Lax, interview with William Packard, *New York Quarterly*, no. 30 (Summer 1986): 26. All subsequent references to this interview appear in the text.

Anderson and American Active Freedom ❑

Reconsidered from the early nineties, Europeans such as Ian Hamilton Finlay and Henri Chopin and Americans such as John Cage, Robert Lax, Kenneth Gaburo, William Burroughs, and Brion Gysin may now be seen as major pioneers of the postmodern multimedia avant-garde. Extending their work within the new media of the eighties, a younger generation of artists such as Steve Reich, Robert Ashley, Yvonne Rainer, Philip Glass, and Robert Wilson, and a still younger generation of artists including Laurie Anderson, Meredith Monk, Kathy Acker, Barbara Kruger, Jenny Holzer, Warren Burt, and Larry Wendt have extended the multimedia aesthetic still further, confirming the prescience of their precursors' experiments and pointing towards what Barthes would term new possibilities "born technically," but "still to be born theoretically."[1]

While contemporary intertextual theory tends to look backwards to the *déjà vu*, and in Jonathan Culler's terms "courts banality" by studying "meanings already known or attested within a culture in the hope of formulating the conventions that members of that culture are following,"[2] the contemporary, multimedia avant-garde might be said to "court" the cutting edge of creativity by identifying and tentatively deploying new kinds of meaning seldom attested or followed within postmodern culture. In Burroughs's terms, *"We are not setting out to explore static pre-existing data.* We are setting out to *create* new worlds, new beings, new modes of consciousness."[3]

Affirming Isabelle Huppert's suggestion that American eyes

now consider Europe as "a sort of Elegant Third World," Baudrillard understandably argues that European cultural supremacy is a mixed blessing, "still at the centre, but at the centre of the Old World," where it lacks the *active freedom* that he perceives "in American institutions and in the head of every citizen."[4] Elsewhere, Baudrillard distinguishes this freedom from "surrealism . . . an extravagance that is still aesthetic in nature and as such very European in inspiration," proposing that it is somehow an aspect of "odd, everyday America."[5]

Laurie Anderson in turn associates this quality with the Bible Belt mentality, locating the origins of her work in a specifically folkloric phenomenon.

> There were people who were just mowing their lawns and doing the most mundane things that you could imagine, and they believed that the oceans parted, and that snakes suddenly appeared on earth. And they would talk about this quite matter-of-factly. . . . I'm just telling the same mixture of mid-Western bible-stories. . . . A mixture of the most mundane things with a twist on them. (interview with author, 30 Jan. 1991)

Specifying that her work is "not surrealistic," but rather, "an incredibly ordinary old chunk of ice," Anderson also insists upon the communicative potential of her performances, irrespective of her use of high technology:

> The latest thing that I did was extremely intimate, and at the same time had this huge amount of high-tech stuff. It was a solo thing. Seventeen people came along on tour for this so-called solo thing. But I felt myself that it was by far the most intimate thing that I've ever done. So it's not a question of size at all. It's a question of how you address people and what you say. Two people can sit at a table, and one can lecture the other in the most formal, remote kind of way you can imagine. And on the other hand, in a group of ten thousand—an audience of ten thousand—one can say something very intimate, in a way that's very intimate, and it will be received that way. There's a whole lot of things that are just not that simple. (interview with author, 30 Jan. 1991)

While Jameson suggests that Anderson's work, like all multimedia work, is very simple and "ought not to have any 'meaning' at all" in the "thematic sense," ("Reading Without Interpretation," 217–18), Anderson would undoubtedly argue that he is "looking for it in the wrong place" and concludes, "I always just wanted to make things that other people could understand. That's my only reason to be here. My only reason" (interview with author, 30 Jan. 1991).

Notes

1. Barthes, "The Third Meaning," 67.
2. Jonathan Culler, *The Pursuit of Signs: Semiotics, Literature, Deconstruction* (Ithaca, N.Y.: Cornell Univ. Press, 1981), 99.
3. William Burroughs, *The Adding Machine: Collected Essays* (London: John Calder, 1985), 102.
4. Baudrillard, *America*, 81.
5. Baudrillard, *America*, 86.

Glass and Wilson: Alienation Effect or Empathy Effect? ❏

Like Laurie Anderson, the American composer Philip Glass similarly stresses the extent to which his notionally fragmentary compositions have the capacity to cohere as "parts of a picture." Somewhat as Cage argues that his *Europera*, "an opera without a libretto," will nevertheless produce surprising theater, Glass insists upon the surprisingly coherent quality of *Einstein on the Beach* (1976), a collaborative opera—or piece of *music theater*—written with the American dramatist Robert Wilson. Specifying that *Einstein on the Beach*, like Cage's *Europera*, lacks any libretto and yet still remained coherent, Glass explains,

> *Einstein on the Beach* . . . is very much based on the principle that an opera—this opera—did not need a libretto, since every-

one brought their own libretto. In other words we depended on the audience to complete the work. . . . We created a musical theater piece based on Einstein in which there is a libretto of fragments, of things that people wrote, but there is no narrative, there's no normal narrative in which a story is told. . . . Unfailingly, people saw this as a libretto about Einstein. Unfailingly.[1]

Robert Wilson's other individual and collaborative productions similarly generate new kinds of music theater and multimedia collage based upon surprisingly positive forms of antinarrative. Rather than producing a Brechtian alienation effect, Wilson's theatrical collage-logic generates an *empathy effect*, or what Stefan Brecht has discussed as "non-verbal, arational communication." Inspired by the autistic behavioral patterns of his collaborator Christopher Knowles, Wilson's productions appear to supplement rational discourse with what one might think of as user-friendly, extrarational, antinarrative. In Stefan Brecht's terms,

Wilson's idea, when rehearsals (and the gathering of the text) started, seemed to be that we, the performers, were to learn from Chris, by talking to and being with him (we were going on tour together), by attempts at communication with him, by imitation of him (imitation would make communication possible). This would within us hollow out/fill out what was to be the show piece of the piece, the form of rational verbal intercourse, would make it vibrate by and would put it in counterpose to a non-verbal, arational communication taking place (so Wilson seemed to suggest) by harmonious sensed reverberation.[2]

Like Cage, Anderson, Glass, and—as we shall see, the cut-up master, William Burroughs—a writer whom Wilson praises particularly because "he's not afraid to destroy the codes in order to make a new language"—Wilson asserts that familiar, rational, linear communication may be supplemented and extended by less familiar modes of arational, extralinear interchange (interview with author, 5 Feb. 1991). As one might always have suspected, communication takes place as we write, speak, listen, and empathize *between the lines* of written, verbal, or gestural statement—a possibility which one can only appreciate if one suspends logical disbelief and accepts that logical communication may be complemented both by illogical *non-communication* and by alternative, extralogical *communication*.

Notes

1. Philip Glass, interview with author, *Review of Contemporary Fiction* 7.2 (Summer 1987): 104, 106.
2. Stefan Brecht, *The Original Theatre of the City of New York: From the Mid-60s to the Mid-70s*, book 1, *The Theatre of Visions: Robert Wilson* (Frankfurt: Suhrkamp Verlag, 1978), 271.

Burroughs, Walker, and the Pattern of Chaos ☐

Even William Burroughs, the creator of cut-ups that he himself dismisses at times as "interesting experimentally, but simply not readable" and that at their most subversive—in *Electronic Revolution* (1971)—are introduced as "a front line weapon to . . . escalate riots," now tempers his enthusiasm for chaotic rhetoric. Responding to the hypothesis that his work emphasizes "images which don't cohere,"[1] Burroughs comments,

> That's a little vague, because images always cohere. By nature, there is a sort of magnetism. You have an image over here, it's going to attract or attach itself to similar images. It's simply a matter of the ways that words work. There's usually a sort of magnetism.[2]

Similarly, when meditating upon Robert Walker's photographs of New York, Burroughs once again emphasizes the potential coherence of the postmodern artist's vision. Pondering upon Walker's evocations of the "unifying unities" within the overpopulated chaos of New York and suggesting that the su-

perficiality of postmodern simulacra may be transpierced by
the percipience of what one might think of as the postmodern
symbolist sensibility, Burroughs advises,

> Now take a stack of photographs . . . you are looking for a point
> where inner and outer reality intersect. . . . Now you don't
> know what intersections the photographer experienced, but if
> he is as good as Walker is, you know he was experiencing
> something quite definite. . . . Walker catches the meaning of
> meaninglessness, the pattern of chaos, the unifying unities of
> disparate elements.[3]

Notes

1. William Burroughs, *The Job: Interview with William Burroughs*, by Daniel Odier (London: Jonathan Cape, 1970), 48; William Burroughs, *Electronic Revolution* (1971), in *Ah Pook Is
Here and Other Texts* (London: John Calder, 1979), 125.

2. William Burroughs, interview with author, 6 Oct. 1983.

3. William Burroughs, "Robert Walker's Spliced New York,"
Aperture, no. 101 (Winter 1965): 66.

Beckett, Warrilow, and the
Clarity of Spirit ❑

Still more surprisingly, perhaps, Samuel Beckett's last works
also approximated this positive postmodern aesthetic when pre-
sented by American companies such as Mabou Mines, shifting
as it were, from evidence substantiating the B-effect to unexpected exemplification of the C-effect. Tracing the ways in
which his reading of *The Lost Ones* gradually became *decentered* from its semantic content and *recentered* upon its sound
and thereby became "incredibly clearer" to both its individual
and collective spectators, the actor David Warrilow comments,

> I don't know what the piece means, *The Lost Ones* . . . it's such
> a mysterious piece. . . . So I decided to drop all my attention to
> sense and try playing the text as if it was a piano concerto, just

dealing with phrasing, and dynamics and just sound. . . . The curious thing was that people who had seen the piece before said, "It's incredibly clearer!"[1]

Turning from the curious success of the New York production of *The Lost Ones* to the still curiouser success of this production's European tour, Warrilow resumes,

> Then I went on to have the experience of performing that piece . . . in France . . . in Italy . . . in Germany. And in all those places, at least for a while, I did it in English only. Nobody *ever* complained that they didn't understand. . . . There's something about the nature of the language, there's something about the clarity of the spirit of it, which makes it comprehensible when people don't understand the words. I can't explain it . . . it's just part of the mystery as far as I'm concerned. (*Review of Contemporary Fiction*, 95–96)

Phrases such as "the mystery," "the clarity of the spirit," "the meaning of meaninglessness," and "the underlying unities of disparate elements" and notions of the effective transfer of meaning and of new theater that one looks forward to experiencing and that the audience will unfailingly complete and understand by responding to harmonious sensed reverberation even when they don't understand the words, come as something of a surprise if one misinterprets the parameters of postmodernism in terms of the misguided assumptions of the B-effect. But viewed from a wider perspective, both in terms of the theories contributing to the B-effect and the theories contributing to the C-effect, it becomes apparent that postmodern culture is far more multifaceted than its critics have usually assumed. As Warrilow tellingly reports, "Nobody *ever* complained that they didn't understand."

Note

1. David Warrilow, interview with author, *Review of Contemporary Fiction* 7.2 (Spring 1987): 95. All subsequent references to this interview appear in the text.

Considered in Diagrammatic Summary: The Phases of Postmodernism ❑

Considered in diagrammatic summary, it might be tentatively postulated that the phases of postmodernism, like those of modernism, fall into three main stages. First, an initial era of apocalyptic panic accompanied by, or succeeded by, a mood of cynical or ludic creativity. Second, a phase of substantial experimentation. Third, a phase of apocalyptic panic accompanied by, or followed by, prophetic confidence in new modes of hybrid creativity.

The early phases of modernism might be exemplified in terms of Max Nordau's *Degeneration* (1895) and the playful decadence of Huysmans's *Against Nature* (1884) and Wilde's *Picture of Dorian Gray* (1891). The second, experimental, phase of modernism may be defined in terms of writings such as Proust's *Swann's Way* (1913), Woolf's *Voyage Out* (1915), and Joyce's *A Portrait of the Artist as a Young Man* (1916). Finally, the third, prophetic phases of modernism culminate in Spengler's "catastrophic" *Decline of the West* (1918 and 1922) and Marinetti's optimistic futurist manifestos.

In its turn, the first phase of postmodernism may be demarcated in terms of Benjamin's mixed feelings regarding the potential of the "'Work of Art in the Age of Mechanical Reproduction" (1936), Brecht's mixed feelings regarding the potential of realist and modernist modes of representation, Sartre's mixed feelings regarding the potential of existence as a whole in *Nausea* (1938), and in terms of such predominantly playful and escapist fictions as Queneau's *The Bark-Tree* (1933) and Beckett's *Watt* (1953).

Postmodernism's second, experimental, phase might be exemplified in terms of more sustained and more substantial "B" productions such as Borges's *Fictions* (1962), Burroughs's *Nova Express* (1964), Barth's *Lost in the Funhouse* (1968), Butor's *La Modification* (1970), Beckett's *Lost Ones* (1970), Ballard's *Atrocity Exhibition* (1970), the *Essential Lenny Bruce* (1972),

Brooke-Rose's *Thru* (1975), and Barthes's *A Lover's Discourse* (1978).

The third, final, and present phase of postmodernism may be defined in terms of the tension between apocalyptic theories such as those of Baudrillard and Jameson (and one might add, apocalyptic fiction such as Don DeLillo's *White Noise* [1984]) and the more optimistic aspirations of Cage and those other multimedia creators that I have associated with the C-effect. The following general tabulation emerges:

The General Phases of Modernism and Postmodernism		
Modernism 1880s–1930s		
1880s–1900s	Catastrophe Theory	Ludic Creativity
1900s–1920s	Substantial Experimentation	
1920s–1930s	Prophetic Pessimism	Prophetic Optimism
Postmodernism 1930s–1990s		
1930s–1950s	Catastrophe Theory	Ludic Creativity
1950s–1970s	Substantial Experimentation	
1970s–1990s	Prophetic Pessimism	Prophetic Optimism

The Modes of Modernism
and Postmodernism ❏

The categories and chronologies outlined in the table are tentatively heuristic rather than definitively historic and to this extent, a revision, vision, and prevision of the contradictory parameters of past, present, and future cultural patterns rather than a precise overview of the last one hundred years. Cage's work obviously does not occur exclusively in the seventies; indeed, as these pages have suggested, the positive creativity of the Cageian project informs postmodern culture from its very inception in the late thirties.

What this chart attempts to suggest, however, is the degree to which both the initial pessimism or superficial play of postmodernists such as Benjamin and Beckett and the more recent hyperpessimism of theorists such as Baudrillard and those other writers that I have associated with the B-effect find their synchronic counterparts in the optimistic aspirations, experimentation, and innovations of creators like Cage and those other postmoderns that I have associated with the C-effect, be they multimedia artists like Glass, Wilson, or Anderson, or born-again symbolists like Burroughs. Briefly, postmodern culture does not simply culminate in the depthless, valueless, centerless trivia that so many of its chroniclers impute to the last thirty or forty years.

Sometimes postmodern compositions disintegrate in accordance with a supposedly Beckettian poetics of failure. Sometimes they disintegrate didactically, in terms of a Brechtian interrogative motivation. Sometimes they lend themselves to diagnosis in terms of Baudrillard's notion of a new form of schizophrenia. And sometimes postmodern creativity comfortably, and comfortingly, confirms Bourdieu's sociological categories, offering little more than banal realist compositions or naive technological or symbolist gestures. Sometimes it rains or shines, in accordance with the predictions of the weather bureau.

But on other occasions, postmodern creativity, like the postmodern climate itself, surpasses the expectations of its keepers. As Burroughs and Warrilow intimate, certain postmodern works appear to break through the Baudrillardian barrier of meaningless simulacra, generating "incredibly clearer" evocations of "the meaning of meaninglessness." And as the multimedia experiments of Cage, Rauschenberg, Anderson, Glass, Wilson, and other postmoderns suggest—and demonstrate to differing degrees—postmodern works concurrently identify, explore, and extend substantial new creative spaces and testify to the continued existence, (r)evolution, and exuberance of the vital avant-garde tradition that postmodernism's pessimistic sages all too easily criticize, rationalize, or fictionalize out of existence.

Baudrillard or Cage? Degeneration or Affirmation? ❏

In its most extreme form, the B-effect in postmodern cultural theory culminates in the Baudrillardian conviction that the sixties and the seventies witness the final throes of the cultural crisis that Baudrillard somewhat nostalgically associates with the era "between Nietzsche and the 1920–1930's" when "people like . . . Benjamin lived through the high point of a culture and the high point of its decline."

In terms of the preceding diagram, Baudrillard never seems to have recovered from the eras of catastrophe theory and prophetic pessimism that I have associated with the 1880s–1900s, the 1920s–1930s, and more recently, the 1970s–1990s. Too old, as it were, to rock n' roll—or place confidence in another cultural revolution—and yet too young to die, he cryptically hints that American culture may perhaps offer a last vestige of hope to his jaded generation: "Today, we see the result of this process of decline and everyone is wondering how to remake a drama out of that. Personally, the only rebound that I found is America."[1] Ultimately, perhaps, there is nothing left for Baudrillard and company to enjoy "after the orgy"—or the orgy *manqué*—of their revolutionary aspirations in the sixties.[2] But that's their problem.

Lyotard's early essays offer more helpful and more hopeful cultural diagnoses. In the same issue of *Musique en jeu* in which Barthes resurrected the author in terms of the grain of the voice, Lyotard's meditations upon "several silences" posit the necessity of a positive, post-Nietzschean music—a music which would not so much evince nonaffirmation and prove "both sickly and healthy like 'the times' " but which would resemble *"the affirmative, the music of Cage"* (emphasis added).[3]

It is precisely this positive postmodern creativity that Cage characteristically champions in "After Antiquity," a recent interview with Peter Gena. Reaffirming his artistic and existential credos, Cage observes,

> Just recently, I finished another installment of the diary *How to Improve the World*. And I put in a statement about the avant-garde, and my belief that there always will be one. I think this, because without the avant-garde, which I think is the flexibility of the mind and the freedom from institutions, theories and laws, you won't have invention and obviously, from a practical point of view, the society needs invention. . . . We must continually invent, as Fuller has said, so as to use less material to produce greater results because of the increase in population. That means that invention is necessary. In the arts, people think that it isn't necessary, but it's equally necessary in order to keep the mind flexible.[4]

To neglect the positive achievements and the flexible aspirations of contemporary artists is to misunderstand, misinterpret, and misalign the parameters of postmodernism and to fall into the Baudrillardian trap of concluding that "Post-Modernism registers . . . the loss of meaning" in a world in which "all that remains is a state of melancholia."[5]

Much more remains, so long as cartographers of contemporary culture distinguish the facts of innovative cultural practice from the fictions of apocalyptic cultural theory. The B-effect thinkers of postmodern culture may well convince themselves that innovation, individuality, and independent creativity are logically impossible. Again, that's their problem. Living and thinking in the nineties, it seems more productive to follow the positive contemporaneity of C-effect thinkers such as Cage, who—like such nineteenth century precursors as Carlyle—defends the mind's capacity to apprehend *Wonder* by looking beyond "logic-mills" grinding out "true causes and effects."[6]

Notes

1. Jean Baudrillard, interview with Catherine Francblin, trans. Nancy Blake, *Flash Art* (international ed.), no. 130 (Oct./Nov. 1966): 55.
2. Baudrillard discusses the difficulty of post-orgiastic initiatives in "What Are You Doing after the Orgy?" trans. Lisa Liebmann, *Artforum* 22.2 (Oct. 1983): 42–46.
3. Jean-François Lyotard, "Plusiers silences," trans. Joseph Maier, in *Driftworks*, by Lyotard (New York: Semiotext(e), 1984), 106. Originally published in *Musique en jeu*, no. 9 (Nov. 1972).
4. John Cage, "After Antiquity," interview with Peter Gena, in *A John Cage Reader*, ed. Peter Gena and Jonathan Brent (New York: C. F. Peters Corp., 1982), 170–71. For criticism of Cage's aesthetic and existential credo, and a kind of anti-C-effect argument, see Cornelius Cardew, "Wiggly Lines and Wobbly Music," *Studio International* 192.894 (Nov./Dec. 1976), 249–55. Here, Cardew dismisses his former enthusiasm for the avant-garde and ponders upon the question of "how to produce and distribute music that serves the needs of the growing revolutionary (political) movement" (249).
5. Baudrillard, *Flash Art*, 55.
6. Thomas Carlyle, "Signs of the Times" (1829), in *Selected Writings*, ed. Alan Shelston (Harmondsworth, Eng.: Penguin, 1971), 78.

Burt, Wendt, and the Positive
Parameters of Postmodernism ☐

> You think I am innarested to hear about your
> horrible old condition? I am not innarested at
> all.
>
> —*William Burroughs*

While B-effect hypotheses initially appear seductive, one rapidly finds that one is "not innarested at all" in the "horrible old condition" of those panic theorists convinced that postmodern culture has finally hit the fan,[1] terminally, terribly, and traumatically. Other, more positive and more informed accounts of postmodern culture's parameters exist, both in the theory and in the practice of happier and more inventive sages such as Cage.

Horrible old conditions are ever with us, but innovative new conditions are equally relevant, if one wishes to understand the temper of past, present, and future times and thereby apprehend the postmodern condition as an ongoing process (rather than as apocalyptically stagnant crisis). Not everybody is destined to contribute to this positive ongoing process. However, all but the most stubborn can at least acknowledge the positive parameters of postmodern culture and can at least partially sympathize with Cage's engaging assertion: "I remain more alive when I make some kind of discovery, than I am doing the same thing over and over. . . . I breathe better, doing something I don't know how to do."[2]

Ultimately, the postmodern condition is what Beckett might call our permanent condition, "where we were, as we were,"[3] confronting the terrors of stasis and decay along with the enchantments of doing something we don't yet know how to do and of making some kind of discovery. All that's different, in other words, is that this process takes place in the present, within all the social, technological, and cerebral transformations that surround us *now*, as opposed to *then*, in the twenties, thirties, forties, fifties, and so on.

As the composer Warren Burt reflects, while it is all too easy to reject both the primitivistic and futuristic innovations animating postmodern culture, it is also possible to defend these impulses the same way that one would defend any other creative endeavor, in terms of their existential responsibility.

> The criticism of the accessing of high technology is that you're simply using the cast-offs of what Allen Ginsberg calls the "suck-ghoul-strangle-death-culture." The criticism of the accessing of world musics is that you're raping the third world for your own petty gain. . . . The reply to the technology question is that since this technology exists, it's up to artists to show that it should be used, that it can be used and that it must be used for peaceful purposes and the expansion of the human spirit. And the reply to the world musics question is that we *are* all in one world now—one planet—and if we choose to be interested in the musics of our neighbours, it is to be hoped that those musics are used with sensitivity and with a political consciousness that respects their point of origin.[4]

Likewise, as the high-tech performance poet Larry Wendt observes, the most innovative developments—such as nanotechnology—will doubtless reincarnate the most familiar existential and creative challenges. Nevertheless, rather than envisaging artists as the inevitable victims of nanotechnology, Wendt suggests,

> I think the people on the forefront will have complete control of it. And there'll be the same kind of problems that we have now, along with commercial overuse of this stuff. I mean the potential for dreck in the whole thing is quite enormous. So you'll have a lot of just really bad, bad stuff, and then you'll have a few who are the real geniuses of the form. I think the majority will be really awful. It should be very interesting, and we'll probably see just the beginnings of that before we go out.[5]

Like Wendt, we might well conclude that many "very interesting" things await our attention "before we go out," as the postmodern condition extends its parameters into the post-postmodern condition.

The mythologies of the postmodern *misadventure* are at most only partial, misanthropic symptoms of the spirit of our times. The reality of the ongoing postmodern *adventure* is far more "innaresting." As Cage reminds us, "We have eyes as well as ears, and it is our business while we are alive to use them" (*Silence*, 199).

Notes

1. William Burroughs, *The Naked Lunch* (1959; rpt. London: John Calder, 1982), 125.

2. John Cage, interview with author, 12 Sept. 1990.

3. Samuel Beckett, *More Pricks Than Kicks* (1966; rpt. London: Calder and Boyars, 1970), 20.

4. Warren Burt, interview with author, 14 Jan. 1991.

5. Larry Wendt, interview with author, 8 Feb. 1991.

Index

Index ❑

Acker, Kathy: critique of Baudrillard, 146–48; and positive work on female sexuality, 147; enthusiasm for Burroughs, 148

Adorno, Theodor: and Beuys, Kuspit, and art after Auschwitz, 62

Amirkhanian, Charles: and multimedia performance, 73; and innovative radio, 95

Anderson, Laurie: and American multimedia C-effect, xi, xii, 22, 54, 73, 145–46, 156–59, 164, 165; and Jameson, 157

Andre, Carl: condemned by Eagleton, 6

Ante-art and anti-art: and Poggioli, 1, 2–3; and modernism, 14; and Cage, 14; Beuys's critique of Duchamp's anti-art, 67

Aragon, Louis: and Wilson, 107; and Buñuel, 138

Architecture: Cage on Fuller, 8–9, 166; Baudrillard on Les Halles, 10; Jameson on lost perspective, 10–11; Cage on glass, 11

Ascott, Roy: and telematics, xii, 52–53, 54

Ashley, Robert: and American multimedia C-effect, xii, 54, 73; *Perfect Lives*, 95–97

Avant-garde: and Cage, xii, 13,

35–36, 78, 165–66; Jameson and Dada, 5; Eagleton and sick joke of postmodern avant-garde, 13–14; impact of modernist avant-gardes, 15, 19, 73, 107; Bürger, Lyotard, Bonito-Oliva, and "end" of, 18–21; Chion, Bourdieu, and phases of, 50–51; Conz and "new saints" of, 76; American initiatives, 97; and classics, 128–29, 152–54; Huyssen, Popper, and "liquidation" of, 130–35; B-effect suspicion of, 137–39

Ballard, J. G.: and Rauschenberg, 37; and television, 142–43; on Baudrillard and "optimistic view," 144

Barthes, Roland: and B-effect, xi, 7, 14; on innovation, 2, 64; on "stupid" systems, 6; on "death of author," 16–17, 87; on *punctum*, 17; on "grain of voice," 40, 166; and Cage, 41–42; and "purist" impulse, 52–53; and Robbe-Grillet, 87; on "third meanings," 114

Baudrillard, Jean: and B-effect, xi, 7, 14, 20; on masses, 8; on Les Halles, 8; on dissolution of reality into "pure simulacrum" and "obscenity," 21; and Robbe-Grillet, 89; on

Index

Cage, John: and C-effect, xii, 8–10, 55–56, 164; and technology, 1, 11–15, 30, 51, 74–75, 78, 103, 134; and Fuller, 8–9, 166; and American antinarrative, 22; and "grin" of text, 27; and Jameson on Rauschenberg, 33–34; on Ryman and the unknown, 34–35, 168, 170; on the avant-garde, 35–36, 77–78, 166; and *Indeterminacy* and performance, 40–44; and Barthes, 41–42; and Beckett, 43–48; and *Europera* and "hybrid" impulse, 54–55; and Feldman, 55–56; and Habermas, 58–59; on Chris Mann, 79; on Beuys's pragmatism, 113; and Indian philosophy, 114; and global culture, 151–52, 154; Lyotard's enthusiasm for, 166; Cardew's criticism of, 167n.4

Cardew, Cornelius: criticism of Cage, 167n.4

Carrà, Carlo: and Cage and technological art, 15

Carrington, Leonora: and surrealist sexism, 109–10; and Ernst, 111; and feminist mythology in *The Hearing Trumpet*, 110–12, 114, 116, 129

C-effect aesthetic, xii, 8–10, 13–14, 15, 39, 48, 54, 55–56, 99, 164

Chadwick, Whitney: and women surrealists, 109–10, 113, 114

Chion, Michel: and Bourdieu and modes of experimental art, 50–51; and "purist" impulse, 52–53; and "hybrid impulse," 53–55

Chopin, Henri: sound poetry and C-effect, xii, 55; Beckett on, 2; and "purist" impulse, 52–53; and Bense, 73, 75; and Cage and technology, 74–75, 78, 103, 107; and innovative radio, 95, 97, 109

Cinema: Chion on experimental phases, 50–55; Mellencamp on Rainer's *The Man Who Envied Women*, 81–82, 90–91, 97; Buñuel on "avantgarde cine," 137–38; Baudrillard on neutralizing screen, 138; DeLillo on "movie-mad" academia, 140

Classics and avant-garde traditions, compatibility of, 128–29, 152–53, 154

Conceptual art: and poststructuralist theory and the "Duchamp heritage," 100

Concrete poetry, 70–72, 79; and modernist avant-garde, 73, 83–84

Conz, Francesco: and "new saints" of avant-garde, 76, 77, 78, 152

Cook, David: and *Panic Encyclopedia*, 141–42

Cubism: and degraded materials, 36; and Robbe-Grillet, 107

Culler, Jonathan: and Burroughs, 155

Dada: Benjamin on, 2, 4; Jameson on, 5; Hitler on, 29; and degraded materials, 36; Janco and postmodernism's two speeds, 83

DeLillo, Don: *White Noise* and cult of crisis, 101; and "trivia-crazed" academia, 140

Derrida, Jacques: and "Duchamp heritage," 100

Index

Index

Index

Utopia: Jameson on exhaustion
of utopian ambition, 10; Buchloh on Beuys's "utopian
drivel," 66, 68, 77; Jappe on
Beuys's "powerful" utopian-
ism, 68–69; Jameson on the
"unacknowledged 'party of
utopia,' " 69–70, 77; Eco on
the need for "readjustment,
fed on utopia," 101; Grass and
the European lack of utopian
confidence, 109; Cage on
Beuys's pragmatic utopian-
ism, 113; Wolf's *Cassandra* as
a "model for a kind of utopia,"
116; Baudrillard, Jameson,
and Ballard's "optimistic view
of America," 144

Varèse, Edgard: and Cage on
the potential of magnetic recording tape, 51
Varo Peret, Remidios: and surrealist sexism, 110
Vautier, Ben: and conceptual
art and the "Duchamp heritage," 100
Video art: and Jameson on Paik
as example of "partial" and
submonumental postmodern
originality, 2–3; Jameson on
the impossibility of video masterpieces, 77; Jameson on the
impossibility of interpreting
video-texts, 139

Walker, Robert: and Burroughs
on photographic images of
"the pattern of chaos," 159–60
Warhol, Andy: cited by Jameson
as examle of "partial" and sub-

monumental postmodern originality, 2–3; and Cage and the
"grin" of the text, 27–28, 56;
and Beckett and "work on leftovers," 28; and Munch's *The
Scream* and Jameson and "institutional" problems, 29–30;
and Rauschenberg and the deconstructive impulse, 37
Warrilow, David: on the "clarity" of Beckett's *Lost Ones,*
160–61, 165
Weill, Kurt: and Hitler and
Reich on the political ineffec-
tiveness of music, 94
Wendt, Larry: and sound poetry,
73; and the potential of nanotechnology, 169–70
Whitelaw, Billie: and Munch
and Beckett's *Footfalls,* 29–30
Wilson, Robert: and collaborations with Müller, xi, 124–29;
and the American C-effect,
xii, 22, 54, 164, 165; praised
by Aragon for realizing the
surrealist dream, 107; and
Shakespeare, 127–28; and the
avant-garde's rediscovery of
the classics, 128–29; and Cage
and Johnson and global culture, 151–52; and Glass and
Einstein on the Beach, 157–
59; admiration for Burroughs,
158; and Knowles and "arational communication," 158
Wolf, Christa: and the European
C-effect, xii, 55, 99; and "third
alternative" to rationalism,
115–17; *Cassandra and Four
Essays,* 116–20; *Cassandra* as
a "model for a kind of utopia,"
116–17; enthusiasm for

Nicholas Zurbrugg is senior lecturer in literary and cultural studies, School of Cultural and Historical Studies, Faculty of Humanities, Griffith University, Brisbane, Queensland, Australia. Educated at the Universities of Neuchâtel, East Anglia, and Oxford, he is the author of *Beckett and Proust* (1988) and *Positively Postmodern—The Multi-Media Muse in America: Interviews with the American Avant-Garde* (forthcoming) and has also published articles on Beckett, Barthes, Baudrillard, Burroughs, Jameson, Dada, Futurism, and the poetics of postmodernism.